without the calories | cakes, cookies and bread
Justine Pattison

For Claire and Cristian, who made it all possible

Also in the *Without the Calories* series

Quick and Easy Without the Calories

Takeaway Favourites Without the Calories

Comfort Food Without the Calories

Pasta and Rice Without the Calories

Easy One Pot Without the Calories

without the calories | cakes, cookies and bread

Justine Pattison

Low-calorie recipes, cheats and
ideas for lighter treats

contents

introduction

MY STORY

I struggled with my weight for years. After being a skinny child and teenager, I piled on the weight during my last years of school and went into my twenties feeling fat and frumpy. A career as a cookery writer and food stylist has helped me understand good food but because my kitchen is always overflowing with great things to eat, temptation is never far away. My weight yo-yoed for 20 years and at my heaviest I weighed more than 15 stone.

A few years ago, I worked on the hit TV series *You Are What You Eat* – I put together those groaning tables of bad food. I also had the chance to work with the contributors on the show, guiding them through the dieting process and helping them discover a whole new way of eating and cooking. Having been overweight myself, I became passionate about helping people lose weight.

Since then, I've worked as a food consultant on many of the weight-loss shows you've seen on TV, and written diet plans and recipes for best-selling books, newspapers and magazines. I'm thrilled that thousands of people have successfully followed my way of cooking and lost weight.

This book, and the others in the *Without the Calories* series, are ideal for anyone who wants to lose weight while leading a normal life. Cooking my way will help you sustain a happy, healthy weight loss. That's what it's all about: you don't have to be stick thin, but you deserve to feel good about yourself. My *Without the Calories* recipes will help you reach your goal.

ABOUT THIS BOOK

Cakes, cookies and breads are so tempting and delicious to eat, but can spell disaster when you are trying to lose weight. In this book, I've created recipes for a variety of treats that contain less fat and sugar than traditional recipes while at the same time keeping them as mouth-watering as possible. When it comes to bread, it's more about the quantity rather than the ingredients so I've kept a close eye on the serving size, and every recipe has been nutritionally calculated so you know exactly what your home-baked goodies contain.

I've also reworked the ingredients and used lots of naturally sweet fruit and vegetables in place of high calorie ingredients, so you'll find that many of the recipes contain more fibre and vitamins too. If you are used to eating sugary confections, the reduction in sweetness can take a little getting used to, but the less sugar you have, the less your body will crave it.

I'm not going to make rash promises about how many pounds you will shed, but I do know that when it comes to losing weight, finding foods that give you pleasure and fit into your lifestyle are the key to success. When you eat well without obsessing over rapid weight loss, it's easier to relax and lose what you need to comfortably – and safely.

To help everyone enjoy these recipes, I've used easy-to-find ingredients and given clear, simple cooking instructions. There's also freezer information where appropriate, so you know which bakes you can store for another day.

If you're already following a diet plan, you'll find additional nutritional information at the back of the book that'll help you work my recipes into your week. And, if you're stuck for inspiration and have a few pounds to lose, try my 123 Plan. It couldn't be easier.

USING THE 123 PLAN

If you're not following a diet regime at the moment and want a great kick-start, try my 123 Plan for a few weeks. I've tried to make it really easy, and you don't need to do too much adding up. You will find over 500 recipes to choose from in my *Without the Calories* series. Just pick one recipe from any section to bring your daily intake to between 900 and 1,200 calories. Add an *essential extra* 300 calories a day and you'll be on your way to a healthy, sustainable weight loss of between 2–3lbs a week.

The recipes in this book are designed to complement the recipes in the other books in the series, or they can be enjoyed as part of your own eating plan. Although they are lower in fat, sugar and calories than traditional recipes, it's best that they aren't eaten every day, but enjoyed every now and then as an extra if you are following the 123 Plan. I'd recommend just once or twice a week for the cakes and cookies, but you can swap the flat breads for rice, pasta or potatoes with meals if you like.

For this reason, they have their own category within the series: *Occasional Extras.*

ONE
up to 300 calories

TWO
300–400 calories

THREE
400–500 calories

*Occasional Extras

There are still recipes in this book that can be used as part of the 123 Plan, including muffins and pizza bakes, but the majority are delicious, alternative ways to enjoy your favourites. If you don't have time to bake, I have put together a list of popular snacks that can also be used as occasional extras (see page 180).

DON'T RUSH IT

Weight tends to be gained over time, and losing it gradually will make the process easier and help give your body, especially your skin, time to adapt. You're more likely to get into positive, enjoyable long-term cooking and eating habits this way too.

WHAT IS A CALORIE?

Put simply, a calorie is a unit of energy contained within food and drink which our bodies burn as fuel. Different foods contain varying amounts of calories and if more calories are consumed than the body needs, the excess will be stored as fat. To lose weight, we need to eat less or use more energy by increasing our activity – and ideally both!

I've provided the calorie content of a single serving of each dish. In my experience, most people will lose at least 2lb a week by consuming around 1,200–1,500 calories a day, but it's always best to check with your GP before you start a new regime. Everyone is different and, especially if you have several stones to lose, you'll need some personalised advice. The calories contained in each recipe have been calculated as accurately as possible, but could vary a little depending on your ingredients.

A few wayward calories here and there won't make any difference to your overall weight loss, but if you have a couple of days eating more than 1,400 calories, try to eat closer to 1,100 for the next few days. Over a week, things will even out.

My recipes strike a balance between eating and cooking well and reducing calories, and I've tried them all as part of my own way of enjoying food without putting on excess weight. Even if you don't need to lose weight, I hope you enjoy cooking from my books simply because you like the recipes.

SECRETS OF SUCCESS

The serving sizes that I've recommended form the basis of the nutritional information on page 182, and if you eat any more, you may find losing weight takes longer. If you're cooking for anyone who doesn't need to watch their calorie intake, feel free to increase their servings, bearing in mind that too much sugar isn't good for anyone.

The right portion size also holds the key to maintaining your weight loss. Use this opportunity to get used to smaller servings. Work out exactly how much food your body needs to maintain the shape that makes you feel great. That way, even when counting calories feels like a distant memory, you'll remain in control of your eating habits.

Balance these occasional treats with mainly healthy, home-cooked meals if you can. Stick to lean protein (which will help you feel fuller for longer) and vegetables and avoid high-fat, high-sugar snacks and confectionery. Be aware that alcohol is packed with empty calories and could weaken your resolve. Starchy carbs such as pasta, rice, potatoes and bread are kept to a minimum because I've found that, combined with eating lots of veg and good protein, this leads to more sustainable weight loss. There's no need to avoid dairy products such as cheese and cream, although they tend to be high in fat and calories. You can swap the high-fat versions for reduced-fat ones, or use less.

Ditch heavily processed foods and you will feel so much better. Switching to more natural ingredients will help your body work with you.

Most recipes in the *Without the Calories* series form the main part of each meal, so there's room to have your plate half-filled with freshly cooked vegetables or a colourful, crunchy salad. This will help fill you up, and boost your intake of vitamins and minerals.

Make sure you drink enough fluids, especially water – around two litres daily is ideal. Staying hydrated will help you lose weight more comfortably, and it's important when you exercise too.

IN THE KITCHEN

Pick up some electronic kitchen scales and a set of measuring spoons if you don't already have them. Both will probably cost less than a takeaway meal for two, and will help ensure good results.

Invest, if you can, in good quality non-stick pans and baking tins. Non-stick baking parchment will prevent sticking and means you need to use less oil. I use oil and butter sparingly, and use a calorie-controlled spray oil for frying. I also keep a jam jar containing a little sunflower oil and a heatproof pastry brush to hand for greasing pans lightly before baking and frying.

STICK WITH IT

Shifting your eating habits and trying to lose weight is not easy, especially if you have been eating the same way for many years. But it isn't too late. You may never have the perfect body, but you can have one that, fuelled by really good food, makes you feel happy and healthy. For more information, tips and ideas, visit www.justinepattison.co.uk.

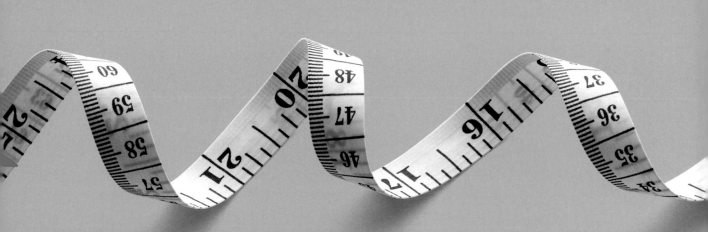

cookies
and biscuits

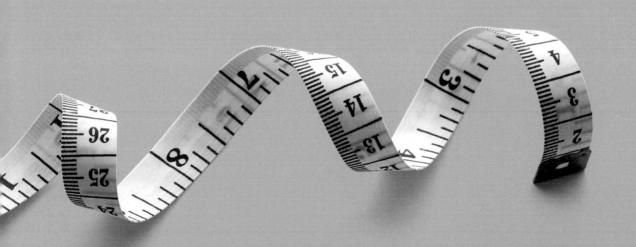

104
CALORIES
PER COOKIE

oaty raisin cookies

MAKES 16
PREP: 15 MINUTES
COOK: 15 MINUTES

200g plain flour
75g porridge oats
  (not jumbo oats)
50g soft light brown sugar
½ tsp baking powder
50g cold butter, cubed
50g raisins
2 medium egg whites
1 tsp vanilla extract

Freeze the cooked and cooled cookies in a freezer-proof container, interleaving them with baking parchment, for up to 3 months. Take out the number of cookies you need and defrost them at room temperature for about an hour before serving.

High fibre oats help make these cookies more satisfying and add a lovely crunch. I've kept sugar levels down but the raisins bring sweetness.

Preheat the oven to 200°C/Fan 180°C/Gas 6. Line 2 baking trays with baking parchment.

Put the flour, oats, sugar and baking powder in a large bowl and rub in the butter until the mixture resembles coarse breadcrumbs. Stir in the raisins. Lightly whisk the egg whites and vanilla until frothy. Then stir them into the flour mixture until evenly combined.

Mix the ingredients with a spoon and then your hands until they come together to form a dough. Divide and roll the dough into 16 small balls. Place the balls on the lined baking trays and press down with your fingers until they are about 5mm deep and 8cm in diameter.

Bake for 15 minutes or until lightly browned and firm. (They will continue to crisp up as they cool.) Cool on the trays for a few minutes then transfer the cookies to a wire rack. Store in an airtight tin for up to 5 days.

56
CALORIES
PER RING

iced rings and chocolate pennies

MAKES 20

PREP: 25 MINUTES

COOK: 20 MINUTES

250g plain flour, plus
   extra for dusting
50g caster sugar
1/4 tsp baking powder
50g cold butter, cubed
2 medium egg whites
1 tsp vanilla extract
20 milk chocolate buttons
   (about 20g)

FOR THE ICING
65g icing sugar, sifted
2–3 tsp cold water
food colouring paste
   (optional)

Two biscuits in one! The iced rings are generous looking enough to fool the eye but the centre has been taken out of each biscuit and dotted with a chocolate button.

Preheat the oven to 200°C/Fan 180°C/Gas 6. Line 2 baking trays with baking parchment.

Put the flour, sugar and baking powder in a large bowl and rub in the butter until the mixture resembles coarse breadcrumbs. Lightly whisk the egg whites and vanilla until frothy. Stir them into the flour mixture and mix the ingredients with a wooden spoon and then your hands until they come together and form a firm, pliable dough.

Roll out the dough on a well floured surface until it is about 2–3mm thick. Sprinkle a little flour under the dough every few rolls and turn the dough in a quarter turn so it doesn't stick.

Use a 9cm plain biscuit cutter to cut out rounds from the dough. Make a hole in the centre of each one with a 5cm cutter and then lift each ring carefully onto the tray. Re-roll the trimmings and continue making biscuits until you have about 20 rings and 20 discs. Bake the rings for 10 minutes or until lightly browned and firm. Cool on the tray for a few minutes then transfer to a wire rack until cold.

To make the icing, mix the icing sugar with 2 teaspoons of the water, adding a few drops extra until smooth and drizzly. Divide into 2 small bowls and stir in a little food colouring, until smooth.

Using a teaspoon, drizzle the icing over the biscuits and leave to set for 30 minutes before serving. If not serving immediately, store the uniced biscuits in an airtight tin for up to 2 weeks. Ice before serving.

Chocolate pennies: While the rings are cooking, press a milk chocolate button into the centre of each little disc. Once the rings are cooling, place the chocolate pennies on the lined trays and bake as above for 9–10 minutes or until lightly browned and firm. Cool on the tray. Makes 20. Calories per biscuit: 26

93
CALORIES
PER COOKIE

coconut cookies

MAKES 16
PREP: 15 MINUTES
COOK: 15 MINUTES

150g plain flour
50g porridge oats
  (not jumbo oats)
50g desiccated coconut
25g soft light brown sugar
½ tsp baking powder
50g cold butter, cubed
2 medium egg whites
1 tsp vanilla extract
1 tbsp semi-skimmed milk

Freeze the cooked
and cooled cookies in a
freezer-proof container,
interleaving them with
baking parchment, for up
to 3 months. Take out the
number of cookies you need
and defrost them at room
temperature for about an
hour before serving.

These cookies are made with just enough coconut to give a lovely flavour and crunch. Sprinkle with a little sifted icing sugar if you like (one teaspoon of icing sugar contains 12 calories).

Preheat the oven to 200°C/Fan 180°C/Gas 6. Line 2 baking trays with baking parchment. (Bake the cookies in batches if you don't have 2 trays.)

Put the flour, oats, 40g of the coconut, sugar and baking powder in a large bowl and rub in the butter until the mixture resembles coarse breadcrumbs. Lightly whisk the egg whites and vanilla until frothy. Then stir them into the flour mixture until evenly combined.

Mix the ingredients with a spoon and then your hands until they come together and form a dough. Divide and roll the dough into 16 small balls. Place the balls on the lined baking trays and press down with your fingers until they are about 5mm deep and 8cm in diameter. Brush the cookies with a little milk and sprinkle with the remaining 10g desiccated coconut.

Bake for 14–15 minutes or until lightly browned and firm. They will continue to crisp up as they cool. Cool on the trays for a few minutes then transfer the cookies to a wire rack. Store in an airtight tin for up to 5 days.

66
CALORIES
PER BISCUIT

chocolate chip biscuits

MAKES 20
PREP: 20 MINUTES,
PLUS COOLING TIME
COOK: 1 HOUR

150g plain flour, plus
    extra for dusting
3 tbsp cocoa powder
25g plain chocolate drops
    (about 50% cocoa solids)
25g white chocolate drops
1 tsp baking powder
75g caster sugar
finely grated zest of
    1 medium orange
1 large egg, plus 1 large
    egg white
½ tsp vanilla bean paste
    or vanilla extract

These chocolate chip biscuits are made in a similar way to Italian biscotti, so they are very crisp but not loaded with fat or sugar. They will last for at least 3 weeks in an airtight jar or tin without softening.

Preheat the oven to 180°C/Fan 160°C/Gas 4. Sift the flour and cocoa powder into a large bowl and stir in the chocolate, baking powder, sugar and orange zest.

Beat the whole egg and egg white with the vanilla and pour onto the flour. Mix with a wooden spoon and then your hands until the ingredients come together and form a stiff but pliable dough.

Transfer the dough to a well floured board and roll it into a fat sausage-shape about 20cm long. Transfer the dough to a large baking tray lined with baking parchment and flatten it slightly until it is about 2cm high.

Bake for 25–30 minutes until the dough is risen and firm but still looks fairly pale. Leave to cool on the baking tray for 10 minutes. Reduce the oven temperature to 140°C/Fan 120°C/Gas 1. Transfer the dough to a board and using a bread knife, cut into roughly 1cm slices.

Return the biscuits to the tray and bake flat for a further 30 minutes or until very lightly browned. The biscuits will become crisp as they dry. Leave to cool, then store in an airtight container for up to 3 weeks.

lemon and white chocolate biscuits

MAKES 20
PREP: 20 MINUTES,
PLUS COOLING TIME
COOK: 1 HOUR

175g plain flour, plus extra
    for dusting
25g white chocolate drops
25g dried chopped
    mixed peel
1 tsp baking powder
75g caster sugar
finely grated zest
    of 2 lemons
1 large egg, plus 1 large
    egg white

Double baking these biscuits means they are extra crisp and light. The mixed peel adds a slightly chewy texture and lots of tangy citrus flavour.

Preheat the oven to 180°C/Fan 160°C/Gas 4. Sift the flour into a large bowl and stir in the chocolate, mixed peel, baking powder, sugar and lemon zest.

Beat the whole egg and egg white together and pour them onto the flour. Mix with a wooden spoon and then your hands until the ingredients come together and form a stiff but pliable dough.

Transfer to a well floured surface and roll into a fat sausage shape about 20cm long. Transfer the dough to a large baking tray lined with baking parchment and flatten it slightly until it is about 2cm high.

Bake for 25–30 minutes until the dough is risen and firm but still looks fairly pale. Leave to cool on the baking sheet for 10 minutes. Reduce the oven temperature to 140°C/Fan 120°C/Gas 1. Transfer the dough to a board and using a bread knife, cut into roughly 1cm slices.

Return the biscuits to the baking tray and bake flat for a further 25 minutes or until very lightly browned. The biscuits will become crisp as they dry. Leave to cool, then store in an airtight container for up to 3 weeks.

31

CALORIES
PER BISCUIT

ginger snaps

MAKES 24
PREP: 20 MINUTES
COOK: 20 MINUTES

115g plain flour, plus
   extra for dusting
¼ tsp bicarbonate of soda
50g soft light brown sugar
2 balls of stem ginger in
   syrup, drained and diced
1 medium egg
3 tsp ground ginger

Ginger snaps are wonderful with a hot cup of tea or coffee and these have all the crunchiness of a traditional biscuit but are lower in fat, helping to reduce the calories.

Preheat the oven to 200°C/Fan 180°C/Gas 6. Line 2 baking trays with baking parchment. Put the flour in a large bowl and stir in the bicarbonate of soda, sugar and stem ginger pieces.

Beat the egg and ground ginger together and pour the mixture onto the flour. Mix with a wooden spoon and then your hands until the ingredients come together and form a stiff dough.

Divide the dough in half and roll out on a well floured surface with a lightly floured rolling pin until the dough is about 2mm thick. Turn the dough every 3–4 rolls, and regularly dust the surface with a little more flour to help prevent it sticking.

Cut the dough into rounds with a 6cm fluted or plain cutter, pressing firmly to cut through the stem ginger. Brush off any excess flour with a dry pastry brush and place the biscuits on the lined baking trays. Re-knead and roll the trimmings until you have made about 24 biscuits.

Bake the biscuits in 2 batches for 10 minutes or until firm and lightly browned. They will continue to crisp up as they cool. Leave them to cool on the tray then pack the biscuits into an airtight container. They should keep well for up to 3 weeks.

58 CALORIES PER COOKIE

white chocolate and cranberry cookies

MAKES 32
PREP: 15 MINUTES
COOK: 15 MINUTES

200g plain flour
75g porridge oats
  (not jumbo oats)
40g white chocolate chips
40g dried cranberries
40g golden caster sugar
½ tsp baking powder
50g cold butter, cubed
2 medium egg whites
1 tsp vanilla extract

Freeze the cooked and cooled cookies in a freezer-proof container, interleaving them with baking parchment, for up to 3 months. Take out the number of cookies you need and defrost them at room temperature for about an hour before serving.

White chocolate and dried cranberries make a luxurious cookie combination. Keep these delicious biscuits in the freezer, so you aren't tempted to eat too many at once.

Preheat the oven to 200°C/Fan 180°C/Gas 6. Line 2 baking trays with baking parchment. (Bake the cookies in batches if you don't have 2 trays.)

Put the flour, oats, chocolate, cranberries, sugar and baking powder in a large bowl and rub in the butter until the mixture resembles coarse breadcrumbs. Lightly whisk the egg whites and vanilla until frothy. Stir this into the flour mixture until evenly combined.

Mix the ingredients with a spoon and then your hands until they come together and form a dough. Divide and roll the dough into 32 small balls. Place the balls on the lined baking trays and press down with your fingers until they are around 3mm deep and about 6cm in diameter – they will rise a little as they cook.

Bake for 15 minutes or until lightly browned and firm. (They will continue to crisp up as they cool.) Cool on the trays for a few minutes, then transfer to a wire rack until cold. Store in an airtight container for up to 5 days.

60
CALORIES
PER COOKIE

maryland-style cookies

MAKES 32
PREP: 15 MINUTES
COOK: 28 MINUTES

200g plain flour
75g porridge oats
(not jumbo oats)
50g soft light brown sugar
½ tsp baking powder
50g cold butter, cubed
40g plain chocolate chips
(about 50% cocoa solids)
25g pecan nuts, roughly
chopped
2 medium egg whites
1 tsp vanilla extract

Freeze the cooked and cooled cookies in a freezer-proof container, interleaving them with baking parchment, for up to 3 months. Take out the number of cookies you need and defrost them at room temperature for about an hour before serving.

If you can't resist a biscuit with your cup of tea, these simple cookies are a great place to start. Great for packed lunches – just store them in the freezer and take out what you need.

Preheat the oven to 200°C/Fan 180°C/Gas 6. Line 2 baking trays with baking parchment

Put the flour, oats, sugar and baking powder in a large bowl and rub in the butter until the mixture resembles coarse breadcrumbs. Stir in the chocolate chips and nuts. Lightly whisk the egg whites and vanilla until frothy. Stir them into the flour mixture until evenly combined.

Mix the ingredients with a spoon and then your hands until they come together and form a dough. Divide and roll the dough into 32 small balls. Place the balls on the lined trays and press them down with your fingers until they are about 5mm deep and about 6cm in diameter.

Bake one tray at a time for 14 minutes or until they are lightly browned and firm. They will continue to crisp up as they cool. Cool on the trays for a few minutes, then transfer to a wire rack. Store in an airtight container for up to 2 weeks.

55
CALORIES
PER RICE CAKE

chocolate rice cakes

MAKES 8
PREP: 5 MINUTES,
PLUS SETTING TIME
COOK: 1–5 MINUTES

40g plain chocolate
(about 50% cocoa solids),
broken into squares
8 unsalted wholegrain rice
cakes (from a packet)

Chocolate-coated rice cakes are expensive to buy and the thick coating means they're fairly high in calories. My version puts you in control. Use shop-bought rice cakes and drizzle them with melted chocolate for a sweet alternative to a chocolate biscuit.

Melt the chocolate in a heatproof bowl set over a saucepan of gently simmering water or in the microwave. Place the rice cakes on a rack over a tray.

Use a teaspoon to drizzle the melted chocolate over the rice cakes. Leave the chocolate to set in a cool place or until solid. Store the rice cakes in an airtight tin, interleaved with baking parchment for up to a week.

25 CALORIES PER BISCUIT

oatcake thins

MAKES 40
PREP: 25 MINUTES
COOK: 25 MINUTES

25g butter
150g fine oatmeal
65g plain flour, plus
   extra for dusting
1/4 tsp baking powder
1/2 tsp fine sea salt
6 tbsp just-boiled water

Freeze the cooked, cooled oatcakes in a freezer-proof container for up to 3 months. Defrost as many as you need at room temperature for about 30 minutes.

Shop-bought biscuits for cheese can be surprisingly high in fat. My oatcake thins are made with just enough fat to add flavour without increasing the calories too much. Serve with small portions of medium-fat cheeses such as Brie, and low-fat cheese with vegetable sticks and fruit to help keep the calories low.

Preheat the oven to 180°C/Fan 160°C/Gas 4. Line 2 baking trays with baking parchment.

Melt the butter in a medium saucepan over a low heat. Mix the oatmeal, flour, baking powder and salt together and stir the mixture into the melted butter. Add the just-boiled water and mix to form a firm but pliable dough.

Turn the dough onto a surface very lightly dusted with flour and divide into 2 portions. This will make it easier to roll out. Knead half the dough into a ball and flatten slightly. Roll out very thinly – just 2mm deep – and cut into rounds with a 11cm plain biscuit cutter.

Cut each oatcake into 4 triangles and place them on a lined baking tray. Knead the trimmings, re-roll and cut again. You should end up with about 10 large oatcakes, each cut into 4 triangles.

Bake the oatcakes, each tray above the other for 25 minutes or until crisp and light golden brown. Swap the trays roughly halfway through the cooking time. They will continue to crisp as they cool. Store in an airtight container for up to 2 weeks.

46
CALORIES
PER BISCUIT

savoury spiced biscuits

MAKES 24
PREP: 20 MINUTES
COOK: 30-35 MINUTES

100g plain flour, plus extra
  for dusting
100g wholemeal plain flour
1 tsp medium curry powder
1 tsp dried chilli flakes
1 tsp cumin seeds
½ tsp fine sea salt
50g cold butter, cubed
1 medium egg
3 tbsp cold water

Freeze the biscuits in a
freezer-proof container for
up to 2 months. Defrost as
many as required at room
temperature for about an
hour before serving.

These little biscuits with their hint of curry and spice are
lower in fat and full in flavour. Spread with low-fat soft cheese
and a sprinkling of fresh chives for a low-calorie snack or
a delicious canapé.

Preheat the oven to 180°C/Fan 160°C/Gas 4. Line a large
baking tray with baking parchment. Put the plain and
wholemeal flour, curry powder, chilli flakes, cumin seeds,
salt and butter in a large bowl and stir lightly.

Using your fingertips, rub the butter into the dry ingredients
until the mixture resembles fine, floury breadcrumbs. Whisk
the egg and water together and stir into the buttery flour.
Mix with a spoon and then bring together in your hands
to form a rough ball.

Place a sheet of baking parchment on the work surface and
put the dough on top. Roll the dough out with a lightly floured
rolling pin until it is about 3mm thick – about the thickness
of a £1 coin. Turn the paper a quarter turn every couple of
rolls. This should prevent it cracking.

Cut the dough into rounds with a 6.5cm fluted or plain cutter
and place the rounds on the baking tray. Re-knead and roll the
trimmings until you have made about 24 biscuits. Use 2 lined
baking trays if necessary.

Bake for 30–35 minutes or until firm and lightly browned.
Leave to cool on the tray then pack into an airtight container.
The biscuits should keep well for up to 2 weeks.

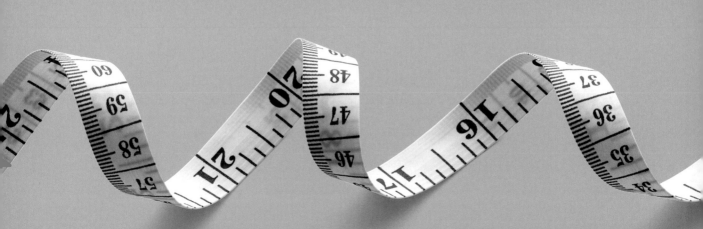

muffins
and scones

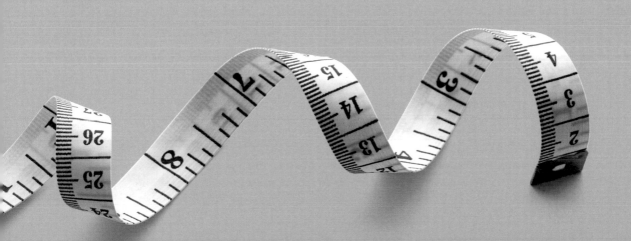

150
CALORIES
PER MUFFIN

mixed berry muffins

MAKES 12
PREP: 10 MINUTES
COOK: 20 MINUTES

1 very ripe medium
 banana (about 100g
 peeled weight)
175ml semi-skimmed milk
3 tbsp sunflower oil
2 large eggs, beaten
1 tsp vanilla bean paste
 or vanilla extract
275g self-raising flour
3 tbsp soft light brown
 sugar
1 tsp bicarbonate of soda
1 small eating apple, peeled
 and coarsely grated
175g frozen mixed berries

Tip: If using squares of
baking parchment (about
12cm squares) grease each
hole a little first and press
the parchment firmly into
the base and the sides.

These fruity muffins make great use of the bags of frozen
berries found in most supermarkets. Use them frozen and
they will thaw as they bake, making a luscious fruity filling
for the muffins. Small berries such as redcurrants and
blueberries work best, so leave out any large strawberries
as they won't defrost quickly enough.

Preheat the oven to 210°C/Fan 190°C/Gas 6½. Line a 12-hole
deep muffin tin with non-stick muffin cases or folded squares
of baking parchment.

Mash the banana with a fork until almost smooth and stir in
the milk, oil, beaten eggs and vanilla.

Sift the flour into a large bowl, add the sugar and bicarbonate
of soda and stir until thoroughly mixed. Make a well in the
centre. Pour the banana mixture onto the flour and mix until
lightly combined. Lightly stir in the grated apple and half the
frozen berries, taking care not to over-mix.

Divide the batter between the muffin cases, top with the
remaining berries and bake for 22–25 minutes or until well
risen and firm. Serve warm or leave to cool on a wire rack.
Store in an airtight container and eat within 2 days. Reheat
the muffins for a few seconds in a microwave oven if you
like, but not for too long or they will toughen.

144
CALORIES
PER MUFFIN

lemon drizzle muffins

MAKES 12
PREP: 15 MINUTES
COOK: 20 MINUTES

oil, for brushing or spraying
2 lemons
2 large eggs
100g Bramley apple sauce
   (from a jar)
100ml semi-skimmed milk
3 tbsp sunflower oil
275g self-raising flour
4 tbsp soft light
   brown sugar
1 tsp bicarbonate of soda

Freeze the cooked and cooled muffins, without icing, in a large freezer bag for up to 1 month. Defrost them at room temperature for about 1 hour and heat for a few seconds in the microwave or for 5 minutes on a baking tray in a moderate oven before serving. If icing, cool for a few minutes before topping.

These zesty muffins can be topped with a lovely drizzly lemon icing and are fabulous served mid-morning with a cup of coffee or tea. Make your own muffin cases with squares of baking parchment if you can – they look great and will peel off the cakes readily.

Preheat the oven to 210°C/Fan 190°C/Gas 6½. Line a 12-hole deep muffin tin with non-stick muffin cases or folded squares of baking parchment. If using squares of baking parchment, grease each hole a little first and press the parchment firmly into the base and sides.

Finely grate the lemon zest, put it in a bowl and beat with the eggs. Cut the lemons in half and squeeze out the juice. You will need about 75ml. (Reserve the rest for the icing.) Add the apple sauce, milk, oil and lemon juice to the eggs and whisk together with a large metal whisk.

Put the flour, sugar and bicarbonate of soda in a large bowl and stir until thoroughly mixed. Make a well in the centre. Pour the lemon mixture onto the flour and mix until lightly combined. It will start expanding as soon as you begin to mix, so it's important to work quickly.

Divide the batter between the muffin cases. Bake for 18–20 minutes or until well risen and firm. Serve warm or leave to cool on a wire rack.

Store the muffins in an airtight container and eat within 2 days. Reheat for a few seconds in a microwave oven if you like, but not for too long or the muffins will toughen.

Runny lemon icing: Mix 100g of sifted icing sugar with about 4 teaspoons of fresh lemon juice until smooth but not too runny. Spoon over the cooled muffins topped with strips of pared lemon zest and set aside for 30 minutes or until just set. Serves 12. Calories per serving: 33

170
CALORIES
PER MUFFIN

chocolate chip muffins

MAKES 12
PREP: 10 MINUTES
COOK: 20 MINUTES

250g vacuum-packed plain
    cooked beetroot (not
    in vinegar), drained
1 very ripe medium
    banana (about 100g
    peeled weight)
200ml semi-skimmed milk
3 tbsp sunflower oil
2 large eggs, beaten
1 tsp vanilla bean paste
    or vanilla extract
50g cocoa powder
250g self-raising flour
4 tbsp soft light
    brown sugar
1 tsp bicarbonate of soda
25g plain chocolate drops
    (about 50% cocoa solids)

Freeze the cooked and
cooled muffins in a large
freezer bag for up to
1 month. Thaw at room
temperature for about
2 hours and heat for a few
seconds in the microwave
or for 5 minutes on a baking
tray in a moderate oven
before serving.

**Deep, dark chocolate muffins look amazing but can contain
a massive number of calories. My version uses grated beetroot
and mashed banana with minimal additional sugar and fat, but
the muffins still have all the rich, chocolatey flavour you'd expect.**

Preheat the oven to 210°C/Fan 190°C/Gas 6½. Line a 12-hole
deep muffin tin with non-stick muffin cases or folded squares
of baking parchment.

Wearing rubber or silicone gloves to protect your hands,
coarsely grate the beetroot, put it in a bowl and set aside.
Mash the banana with a fork until almost smooth and stir
in the milk, oil, beaten eggs and vanilla.

Sift the cocoa into a large bowl. Add the flour, sugar and
bicarbonate of soda and stir until thoroughly mixed. Make
a well in the centre. Pour the banana mixture onto the flour
and mix until lightly combined. Lightly stir in the beetroot,
taking care not to over-mix.

Divide the batter between the muffin cases, sprinkle each
one with chocolate drops and bake for 20 minutes or until well
risen and firm. Serve warm or leave to cool on a wire rack. Store
in an airtight container and eat within 2 days. Reheat for a few
seconds in a microwave oven if you like, but not for too long
or the muffins will toughen.

157
CALORIES
PER MUFFIN

apple and raisin muffins

MAKES 12
PREP: 15 MINUTES
COOK: 20 MINUTES

1 very ripe medium
   banana (about 100g
   peeled weight)
225ml semi-skimmed milk
3 tbsp sunflower oil
2 large eggs, beaten
2 small eating apples
275g self-raising flour
1 tsp ground mixed spice
3 tbsp soft light
   brown sugar
1 tsp bicarbonate of soda
40g raisins

Freeze the cooked and
cooled muffins in a large
freezer bag for up to
1 month. Defrost them
at room temperature for
about an hour and heat
for a few seconds in the
microwave or for 5 minutes
on a baking tray in a
moderate oven before
serving.

Tip: If using bought muffin
cases, you'll find that
straight tulip-shaped cases
will peel off more easily.

Tender pieces of apple, banana and succulent raisins make
these spicy muffins taste sweet, although added sugar is
kept to a minimum. Great for packed lunches and they also
freeze beautifully.

Preheat the oven to 210°C/Fan 190°C/Gas 6½. Line a 12-hole
deep muffin tin with non-stick muffin cases or folded squares
of baking parchment.

Mash the banana with a fork until almost smooth and stir
in the milk, oil and beaten eggs. Peel, quarter and core the
apples and cut them into small chunks.

Put the flour, spice, sugar and bicarbonate of soda in a large
bowl and stir until thoroughly mixed. Make a well in the centre.
Pour the banana mixture onto the flour and mix until lightly
combined. Stir in the apples and raisins.

Divide the batter between the muffin cases and bake for
18–20 minutes or until well risen and firm. Serve warm or leave
to cool on a wire rack. Store in an airtight container and eat
within 2 days. Reheat for a few seconds in a microwave oven
if you like, but not for too long or the muffins will toughen.

172
CALORIES
PER MUFFIN

breakfast muffins

MAKES 12

PREP: 15 MINUTES

COOK: 20 MINUTES

1 very ripe medium
   banana (about 100g
   peeled weight)
200ml semi-skimmed milk
3 tbsp sunflower oil
2 large eggs, beaten
finely grated zest of
   1 orange
4 tbsp fresh orange juice
250g self-raising flour
3 tbsp soft light
   brown sugar
1 tsp bicarbonate of soda
5 tbsp porridge oats, plus
   2 tsp (not jumbo oats)
50g ready-to-eat dried
   apricots, snipped into
   quarters
50g ready-to-eat dried
   stoned prunes, snipped
   into quarters
1 tbsp mixed sunflower
   and pumpkin seeds

Freeze the cooked and
cooled muffins in a large
freezer bag for up to
1 month. Defrost them
at room temperature for
about an hour and heat
for a few seconds in the
microwave or for 5 minutes
on a baking tray in a
moderate oven before
serving.

All the ingredients of a healthy breakfast squeezed into a light, fluffy muffin. Great for taking to work, these muffins freeze well and can be warmed in the microwave or a hot oven before serving.

Preheat the oven to 210°C/Fan 190°C/Gas 6½. Line a 12-hole deep muffin tin with non-stick paper cases or folded squares of baking parchment.

Mash the banana with a fork until almost smooth and stir in the milk, oil, beaten eggs, orange zest and juice.

Put the flour, sugar, bicarbonate of soda and 5 tablespoons of oats in a large bowl and stir until thoroughly mixed. Make a well in the centre. Pour the banana mixture onto the flour and mix until lightly combined. Stir in the apricots and prunes but take care not to over-mix.

Divide the batter between the muffin cases, sprinkle with the remaining porridge oats and mixed seeds. Bake for 18–20 minutes or until well risen and firm. Serve warm or leave to cool on a wire rack. Store in an airtight container and eat within 2 days. Reheat for a few seconds in a microwave oven if you like, but not for too long or the muffins will toughen.

219
CALORIES
PER SCONE

raspberry scones

MAKES 6
PREP: 10 MINUTES
COOK: 15 MINUTES

250g self-raising flour,
   plus extra for dusting
40g butter, plus extra
   for greasing
1 tbsp caster sugar
125ml semi-skimmed milk,
   plus extra for brushing
75g frozen raspberries
   (not defrosted)

Freeze the cooked and cooled scones in a freezer bag for up to 3 months. To serve, place the frozen scones on a baking tray and reheat in a preheated oven at 190°C/Fan 170°C/Gas 5 for 6–8 minutes. Alternatively, defrost the scones at room temperature for 1 hour then warm them in a microwave oven on full power for 20–30 seconds.

Making scones with frozen raspberries means you don't have to use as much, if any, jam. Serve warm with half-fat crème fraiche or extra-thick single cream instead of high-fat clotted cream.

Preheat the oven to 220°C/Fan 200°C/Gas 7. Line a large baking tray with baking parchment. In a large mixing bowl, rub the flour, butter and sugar together, using your fingertips, until the mixture resembles breadcrumbs.

Make a well in the centre of the flour and slowly add the milk, stirring continuously until the mixture comes together and forms a light, spongy dough. Knead in the frozen raspberries until evenly distributed. Turn the dough onto a well-floured surface and press with the palms of your hands or a rolling pin until it is roughly 2cm thick.

Using a 6cm round plain biscuit cutter, cut 4 rounds from the dough and place them on the prepared baking tray, spacing them well apart. Knead again, then press or roll the trimmings and cut 2 more rounds from the dough. Cut the dough cleanly and avoid squidging or dragging for the best rise.

Brush the tops of the scones with a little milk or beaten egg and bake in the centre of the oven for 15–17 minutes or until well risen and golden brown. Remove from the oven and serve warm or cold with half-fat crème fraiche, extra-thick single cream or a scraping of butter (but don't forget to add the extra calories).

135
CALORIES
PER SERVING

potato scones

SERVES 4
PREP: 10 MINUTES
COOK: 30 MINUTES

250g floury potatoes
    (about 1 large), peeled
    and cut into roughly
    4cm chunks
25g butter
½ tsp fine sea salt
50g self-raising flour,
    plus extra for dusting

Freeze the cooked and cooled scones in a freezer-proof container, interleaved with baking parchment, for up to 1 month. Reheat from frozen on a baking tray in a preheated oven at 180°C/Fan 160°C/Gas 4 for 10 minutes before serving.

Floury potatoes such as King Edwards or Maris Pipers should be used for these Irish potato scones. Serve warm with a little butter or instead of toast with grilled back bacon, tomatoes and poached eggs.

Place the potato chunks in a medium saucepan and cover with cold water. Bring to the boil, then reduce the heat to a simmer and cook for about 15 minutes or until the potato is very soft but not mushy. Drain well in a colander and return to the saucepan.

Mash the potato with the butter and salt until smooth. Beat in the flour with a wooden spoon until the mixture forms a thick dough that does not stick to the sides of the saucepan. Turn onto a lightly floured surface and roll into a large ball. Flatten the dough into a round roughly 20cm in diameter. Cut into 8 wedges.

Heat a large flat griddle or heavy-based, non-stick frying pan over a medium heat. Cook the scones in batches for 2–3 minutes on each side or until golden brown and firm. Keep the first batch warm by wrapping it in a clean tea towel or napkin while you cook the second.

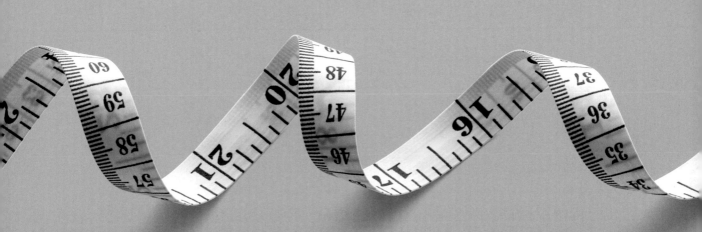

tea-time
cakes

27
CALORIES
PER CAKE

chocolate crispy cakes

MAKES 12
PREP: 10 MINUTES,
PLUS CHILLING TIME
COOK: 1½–5 MINUTES

25g plain chocolate (about
   50% cocoa solids) or milk
   chocolate drops
50g puffed rice cereal
   (such as Rice Krispies)

These are always a favourite with children. I've cut out the syrup and butter from my recipe and kept chocolate to a minimum. Use squares taken from a chocolate bar instead of drops if you like, but don't pick one containing high cocoa solids as the flavour could be too overpowering and the calories will be higher.

Melt the chocolate in a medium heatproof bowl in the microwave or over a pan of gently simmering water. Take off the heat and stir until smooth. Line a 12-hole cake tin with paper fairy cake cases (not muffin cases).

Stir the puffed rice into the melted chocolate until they are well combined then spoon the mixture into the prepared tin, dividing it as evenly as possible between the cake cases. Put the tin in the fridge and chill for about an hour or until the cakes are solid.

167
CALORIES
PER SERVING

carrot cake with soft cheese frosting

SERVES 12
PREP: 15 MINUTES
COOK: 30–35 MINUTES

oil, for brushing or spraying
300g carrots, peeled and
    coarsely grated (about
    265g prepared weight)
50g sultanas
finely grated zest of
    1 medium orange
250g self-raising flour
3 tsp ground mixed spice
1 tsp bicarbonate of soda
50g butter
25g soft brown sugar
100ml semi-skimmed milk
2 large eggs, beaten

TOPPING
250g quark (fat-free soft
    cheese), drained
1 tbsp icing sugar, sifted

Freeze the cooked and
cooled cake without the
icing, wrapped in foil and
placed in a freezer bag for
up to 2 months. Unwrap and
thaw at room temperature
for about 3 hours then top
with the icing.

Tip: The quark topping for
this cake contains about
18 calories per serving. See
page 56 for how to make
your own at home.

A simple mix and bake cake flavoured with mixed spices
and topped with quark. Quark can be found with other soft
cheeses in larger supermarkets – it is similar to cream cheese
but doesn't contain fat, so the calories are reduced.

Preheat the oven to 180°C/Fan 160°C/Gas 4. Grease and line
the base of a 23cm spring-clip cake tin with baking parchment.
Put the grated carrots, sultanas and orange zest in a large bowl,
add the flour, spice and bicarbonate of soda and toss together.
Make a well in the centre.

Put the butter and sugar in a medium saucepan. Melt together
over a low heat, stirring regularly. Take the saucepan off the
heat and stir the milk into the hot syrup mixture, then add
the beaten eggs, stirring vigorously.

Pour gradually into the flour mixture, stirring continuously
with a wooden spoon to form a thick batter. Pour the batter
into the prepared tin. Bake in the centre of the oven for 30–35
minutes or until the cake is risen and firm to the touch and
a skewer inserted into the centre comes out clean. Leave
to cool in the tin.

Take the cake out of the tin and peel off the baking parchment.
Place the cake on a board or plate. To make the topping, mix
the quark lightly with the sifted icing sugar and spread it over
the cake. If you can't find quark, use light soft cheese or dust
the cake with sifted icing sugar – but adjust the calories
accordingly. Keep in the fridge and eat within 3 days.

160
CALORIES
PER SERVING

coffee maple pecan cake

SERVES 16
PREP: 20 MINUTES
COOK: 30 MINUTES

oil, for brushing or spraying
400g parsnips, peeled
 and finely grated (about
 300g prepared weight)
250g self-raising flour
1 tsp bicarbonate of soda
3 tbsp instant coffee
 granules
1½ tbsp just-boiled water
2 large eggs, beaten
100g maple syrup
5 tbsp sunflower oil
100ml semi-skimmed milk

TOPPING
2 tsp instant coffee granules
4 tsp just-boiled water
100g icing sugar, sifted
15g shelled pecan nuts,
 roughly broken

Freeze the cooked and
cooled cake without the
icing, wrapped in foil and
placed in a large freezer bag
for up to 2 months. Unwrap
and defrost at room
temperature for about
3 hours before icing.

This cake has a secret ingredient – grated parsnips. They help make it sweet and light and the rich coffee flavour complements them perfectly. No one will ever know – unless you tell them.

Preheat the oven to 190°C/Fan 170°C/Gas 5. Grease and line the base of a 20cm square cake tin with baking parchment. Put the grated parsnip in a large bowl and add the flour and bicarbonate of soda. Rub them into the parsnips with your fingertips as if you were rubbing fat into flour to make pastry. Make a well in the centre.

Put the coffee in a small bowl and stir in the just-boiled water until the coffee dissolves. Beat the eggs, maple syrup, oil, milk and coffee mixture together until thoroughly combined.

Pour the coffee mixture slowly onto the flour mixture, stirring continuously with a wooden spoon to form a thick batter. Pour the batter into the prepared tin and make a wide, shallow dip in the centre with the back of a spoon. (This should stop the cake rising too much in the middle.)

Bake for 30–35 minutes or until the cake is well risen and firm to the touch. Leave to cool in the tin for 5 minutes then turn it out onto a wire rack, peel off the baking parchment and leave to cool.

To make the icing, dissolve the coffee in the just-boiled water in a small bowl and leave to cool completely. Stir the coffee liquid into the icing sugar and mix to form a smooth, fairly thick paste. If the icing is too thick to spread, add a few drops of cold water.

Spoon the icing on top of the cake and spread it to the sides with a palette knife or the back of a spoon. Sprinkle with the pecan nuts and leave to set for at least 30 minutes before cutting into small squares to serve.

caramel cakes with vanilla frosting

MAKES 12
PREP: 25 MINUTES
COOK: 18–20 MINUTES

50g butter
50g golden syrup
200g self-raising flour
1 tsp bicarbonate of soda
2 medium eggs, beaten
1 tsp vanilla extract
2 firm but ripe pears
   (each about 175g)

FROSTING
150g quark (fat-free soft
   cheese), drained
15g sifted icing sugar
1 tsp vanilla bean paste
   or extract

Tip: You can make your own quark by straining fat-free fromage frais through a sieve – it works brilliantly and can be used for any of the frostings in this book (see recipe, right).

These cakes contain less than half the butter I would normally use but the grated pears help to keep them deliciously moist. The caramel flavour comes from the golden syrup – it contains fewer calories gram for gram than caster sugar, but imparts sweetness throughout the sponge.

Preheat the oven to 190°C/Fan 170°C/Gas 5. Line a 12-hole cake tin with paper fairy cake cases. Put the butter and syrup in a medium saucepan. Melt them together over a low heat, stirring regularly. Take the saucepan off the heat and leave to cool. Put the flour and bicarbonate of soda in a large bowl and toss them well together. Make a well in the centre.

Beat the eggs and vanilla together and add them to the butter and syrup mixture, stirring vigorously. Peel and coarsely grate the pears (you will need about 225g of grated pear) and stir them into the egg mixture.

Pour the pear mixture gradually into the flour, stirring continuously with a large metal spoon to form a thick batter. Divide the mixture between the cake cases. Bake in the centre of the oven for 16–18 minutes or until the cakes are risen and firm to the touch. Transfer carefully to a wire rack to cool.

To make the frosting, put the quark in a bowl and stir in the sifted icing sugar and vanilla.

Spoon the frosting onto each cake and swirl with a small palette or table knife. Serve at once or put them in a lidded container and store in the fridge for up to 2 days.

Home-made quark: Put 500g of fat-free fromage frais in a fine sieve and place the sieve over a bowl. Cover and leave to drip overnight in the fridge or until about 175ml of liquid has seeped from the fromage frais. Makes about 325g. Calories per 100g: 49

161
CALORIES
PER CAKE

little banoffee cakes

MAKES 12
PREP: 20 MINUTES,
PLUS STANDING TIME
COOK: 16–18 MINUTES

50g butter
50g golden syrup
175g self-raising flour
½ tsp bicarbonate of soda
2 large eggs, beaten
1 tsp vanilla extract
2 very ripe bananas (about
    200g peeled weight)

DECORATION
65g golden icing sugar,
    sifted
2 tsp water
20g fudge pieces or dairy
    fudge cut into tiny cubes
12 dried banana chips

Freeze the cooked and
cooled cakes, without icing,
in a freezer-proof container,
interleaving them with
baking parchment for up
to 1 month. Take out the
number of cakes you need,
remove the paper cases
and defrost them at room
temperature for about
30 minutes before icing.

Banana and toffee flavours make a fantastic combination for these lovely little cakes.

Preheat the oven to 190°C/Fan 170°C/Gas 5. Line a 12-hole cake tin with paper fairy cake cases. Put the butter and syrup in a medium saucepan. Melt them together over a low heat, stirring regularly. Take the saucepan off the heat and leave to cool. Put the flour and bicarbonate of soda in a large bowl and toss them well together. Make a well in the centre.

Beat the eggs and vanilla together and add them to the butter and syrup mixture, stirring vigorously. Peel and mash the bananas in a bowl with a fork until almost smooth and stir them into the egg mixture.

Pour the wet ingredients gradually into the flour mixture, stirring continuously with a wooden spoon to form a thick batter. Spoon the batter into the cake cases. Bake in the centre of the oven for 15–18 minutes or until the cakes are risen and firm to the touch. Leave to cool on a wire rack.

To make the icing, mix the sifted icing sugar with 2 teaspoons of water, adding a few extra drops extra, until smooth and drizzly. Using a teaspoon, drizzle the icing over the cupcakes. Stand for 10 minutes, then scatter with fudge pieces and place a banana chip on top. Leave to set for at least 30 minutes before serving.

188
CALORIES
PER SERVING

ginger cake with drizzly lime icing

SERVES 12
PREP: 20 MINUTES
COOK: 40 MINUTES

oil, for brushing or spraying
2 medium courgettes,
  trimmed and finely grated
  (about 325g prepared)
250g self-raising flour
1 tsp bicarbonate of soda
50g butter
50g golden syrup
150ml semi-skimmed milk
2 large eggs, beaten
2 tbsp ground ginger
50g black treacle

LIME ICING
100g icing sugar, sifted
4 tsp fresh lime juice
20g crystallized ginger,
  roughly chopped
finely chopped zest of
  1 lime (optional)

Freeze the cooked and cooled cake without the icing, wrapped in foil and placed in a large freezer bag for up to 2 months. Unwrap and defrost at room temperature for about 3 hours before icing.

My ginger cake is just as moist and gingery as a classic recipe. I've kept the butter, treacle and golden syrup as low as possible and used grated courgette instead. Don't worry, you won't taste the courgettes once the cake is baked!

Preheat the oven to 190°C/Fan 170°C/Gas 5. Grease a 25cm ring-shaped cake tin and line the base with a ring of baking parchment. Squeeze the grated courgettes over the sink to remove excess water and put them in a large bowl.

Add the flour and bicarbonate of soda and rub them into the grated courgettes with your fingertips as if you were rubbing fat into flour to make pastry. Make a well in the centre.

Put the butter and syrup in a medium saucepan. Melt together over a low heat, stirring regularly. Take the saucepan off the heat and stir the milk into the hot syrup mixture, then add the beaten eggs, stirring vigorously.

Slowly add the mixture to the bowl with the grated courgette, stirring with a wooden spoon to form a thick batter. Pour the batter into the prepared tin and bake in the centre of the oven for 35–40 minutes or until the cake is well risen, firm to the touch and a skewer inserted into the thickest part of the cake comes out clean. Leave to cool in the tin.

To make the icing, sift the icing sugar in a bowl and stir in enough lime juice to make a smooth, drizzly icing. Loosen the sides of cake with a round-bladed knife and take it out of the tin. Peel off the baking parchment.

Place it on a cake stand or plate and spoon the icing slowly over the top and allow it to drizzle down the sides. Top with the ginger pieces and lime zest, if using. Stand for at least 30 minutes before cutting. Eat within 3 days or freeze after cooling.

123

CALORIES
PER CAKE

little eccles cakes

MAKES 12
PREP: 20 MINUTES
COOK: 30 MINUTES

320g ready-rolled
   reduced-fat puff pastry
1 tsp plain flour, for dusting
1 medium egg white
2 tsp caster sugar

FILLING
10g butter
1 small eating apple, peeled
   and coarsley grated,
   discarding the core
100g mixed dried fruit
heaped 1/4 tsp ground
   mixed spice
finely grated zest of
   1/2 lemon

Freeze the cooked and cooled Eccles cakes in a large freezer bag for up to 2 months. Defrost at room temperature for about 1 hour before serving or reheat from frozen on a baking tray in a preheated oven at 190°C/Fan 170°C/Gas 5 for 10 minutes.

Eccles cakes don't have to be loaded with calories. I've made mine with reduced-fat puff pastry and a naturally sweet filling with grated apple and dried fruit. If you can't find reduced-fat pastry, make them with normal puff pastry but add an extra 13 calories to each cake.

To make the filling, gently melt the butter in a non-stick saucepan and stir in the grated apple, mixed dried fruit, spice and lemon zest. Cook for 2–3 minutes, stirring over a medium heat until the apple is slightly softened. Remove from the heat and set aside to cool. Preheat the oven to 200°C/Fan 180°C/Gas 6. Line a large baking tray with baking parchment.

Unroll the pastry onto a lightly floured surface and cut it into 8 or 9 circles using a 9cm plain biscuit cutter. Stack the trimmings on top of each other without kneading (this will help keep all the layers) and re-roll with a rolling pin until it is about 3mm thick. Cut out a further 3–4 discs. Lightly whisk the egg white until slightly frothy.

Take a disc and place it in the palm of your hand. Place a tablespoon of the filling mixture in the centre of each disc. Brush the edge of the pastry circle very lightly with the egg white.

Bring the pastry up around the filling and press the edges together very firmly to form a little purse. Turn it over and flatten it between your hands until it is about 1.5cm thick. Place on the lined baking tray and score the surface 3 times with a knife. Repeat the same process to make the remaining 11 Eccles cakes. (You may not need all of the filling.)

Brush all the Eccles cakes with more beaten egg white and sprinkle over a little caster sugar. Bake in the centre of the oven for 18–20 minutes or until risen and golden brown. Cool for a few minutes then serve warm or cold.

142
CALORIES
PER SERVING

strawberry jam swiss roll

SERVES 8
PREP: 20 MINUTES
COOK: 12 MINUTES

oil, for brushing or spraying
3 large eggs
75g caster sugar, plus 2 tsp
1 tsp vanilla extract
100g plain flour
125g reduced-sugar
   strawberry jam,
   well stirred

Freeze the cooked and cooled cake wrapped in foil and placed in a large freezer bag for up to 3 months. Unwrap and defrost at room temperature for about 1 hour before serving.

Whisked sponge mixtures rely on the combination of air, eggs and sugar to make them light and can be made without added fat. Make sure you whisk the eggs and sugar well at the beginning and roll the sponge while it's still warm so it doesn't crack.

Grease and line the base and sides of a 33 x 23cm Swiss roll tin with baking parchment. Preheat the oven to 200°C/Fan 180°C/Gas 6. Put the eggs, 75g of caster sugar and the vanilla in a large bowl and whisk using an electric whisk until the mixture is pale, very light and thick enough to leave a trail when the whisk is lifted. This will take 3–4 minutes.

Sift over half the flour, then use a large metal spoon to lightly fold it into the egg mixture. Sift over the remaining flour and fold it in. It's important to use gentle movements to retain as much air as possible; watch out for pockets of flour.

Pour the mixture slowly into the prepared tin and gently spread with a spatula, so the base of the tin is evenly covered. Bake for 11–12 minutes or until well risen, pale golden brown and firm to the touch. When ready, the cake should begin to shrink away from the sides of the tin and if you touch the centre of the sponge it should spring back immediately.

While the sponge is cooking, place a damp tea towel on the work surface and cover it with a sheet of baking parchment. Sprinkle it with the remaining sugar. Working quickly, turn the cake out onto the sugared paper and carefully remove the baking parchment. Make sure the short side of the cake is facing you.

Using a sharp knife, cut thin strips of the crusty edges from the long sides. Score across the sponge lightly about 2.5cm from the bottom. This will help make a tight turn when you roll the sponge, but make sure you only cut half way through it.

Immediately spread the sponge all over with the jam and roll from the scored end, starting with a tight turn to make a good round shape. Most of the sugar will drop off. Leave to cool on a wire rack then place on a serving plate. Cut into slices and serve.

double chocolate swiss roll

SERVES 8
PREP: 20 MINUTES
COOK: 12 MINUTES

oil, for brushing or spraying
75g plain flour
15g cocoa powder
3 large eggs
75g caster sugar
125g reduced-sugar jam,
   ideally cherry, well stirred
15g white chocolate drops
15g plain chocolate drops
   (about 50% cocoa solids)

Freeze the cooked and cooled cake without the chocolate decoration, wrapped in foil and placed in a large freezer bag for up to 3 months. Unwrap and defrost at room temperature for about 1 hour before decorating and serving.

This cake contains no added fat, so you can fill it with reduced-sugar jam and drizzle it with melted chocolate and still keep the calories low.

Grease and line the base and sides of a 33 x 23cm Swiss roll tin with baking parchment. Preheat the oven to 200°C/Fan 180°C/Gas 6. Sift the flour and cocoa powder together. Put the eggs and sugar in a large bowl and whisk using an electric whisk until the mixture is pale, very light and thick enough to leave a trail when the whisk is lifted. This will take 3–4 minutes.

Sift half the flour and cocoa powder over the egg mixture, then use a large metal spoon to lightly fold in. Sift over the remaining flour and cocoa and fold in. Use gentle movements to retain as much air as possible but watch out for pockets of flour.

Pour the mixture slowly into the tin and gently spread with a spatula, so the base of the tin is evenly covered. Bake for 11–12 minutes or until well risen and firm. The cake should be beginning to shrink away from the sides of the tin and the centre of the sponge it should spring back immediately when touched.

Place a damp tea towel on the work surface and cover it with a sheet of baking parchment. Working quickly, turn the cake out and remove the paper. Make sure the short side is facing you.

Using a sharp knife, cut thin strips of the crusty edges from the long sides. Score across the sponge lightly about 2.5cm from the bottom, but make sure you only cut half way through it. Immediately spread the sponge with the stirred jam and roll up from the scored end, starting with a tight turn to make a good round shape. Leave to cool on a wire rack.

Put the chocolate drops in separate heatproof bowls and melt in the microwave or over pans of simmering water. Take off the heat and stir until smooth. Using teaspoons, drizzle the melted chocolate over the cake and down the sides.

Place in the fridge for about 30 minutes or until the chocolate has set, then place the cake on a serving plate or board. Cut into slices and serve.

56

madeleines

MAKES 12
PREP: 10 MINUTES
COOK: 7–8 MINUTES

oil, for brushing or spraying
2 large eggs
50g caster sugar
1 tsp vanilla bean paste
   or vanilla extract
75g plain flour

Freeze the cooked
and cooled madeleines
individually in foil and
place them in a freezer
bag. Freeze for up to
3 months. Unwrap while
frozen and defrost at room
temperature for about
30 minutes before serving.

Tip: Madeleine tins are
available in cook shops,
department stores
and online. They are a
worthwhile investment if
you like baking but, like
me, find the idea of portion
control really useful.

**These little vanilla cakes are perfect for lunch boxes
if wrapped individually in foil and frozen. Serve simply
with a cup of tea or add fresh berries or a mixed fruit
salad for a quick dessert.**

Preheat the oven to 200°C/Fan 180°C/Gas 6. Lightly
grease a 12–14 hole non-stick madeleine tin.

Put the eggs, sugar and vanilla in a medium bowl and whisk
using an electric whisk until the mixture is pale, creamy and
thick enough to leave a trail when the whisk is lifted – this
should take 3–4 minutes.

Sift over half the flour and use a large metal spoon to lightly
fold the flour into the egg mixture. Sift over the remaining flour
and fold it in. It's important to use gentle movements to retain
as much air as possible in the batter, but you'll need to watch
out for pockets of flour.

Carefully spoon the batter into the madeleine tin. If your tin
is very shallow, you may not need all the batter and can bake
a couple of extra cakes once the first batch is done.

Bake for 7–8 minutes until well risen, pale golden brown and
firm to the touch. Depending on your tin, the madeleines may
be easier to remove when cooled.

172
CALORIES
PER CAKE

mary's rock cakes

MAKES 8

PREP: 10 MINUTES

COOK: 15 MINUTES

200g self-raising flour
50g cold butter, cubed
25g caster sugar, plus 1 tsp
50g mixed dried fruit
1 medium egg
1 tbsp milk

Freeze the cooked and cooled rock cakes in a large freezer bag for up to 2 months. Defrost them at room temperature for 1 hour. Warm through on a baking tray in a moderate oven for 5–10 minutes or for a few seconds in the microwave.

Some of the quickest and simplest cakes you'll ever make. I've reduced the sugar and fat and made them a bit smaller than my usual recipe, but they're so delicious no one will complain.

Preheat the oven to 200°C/Fan 180°C/Gas 6. Line a large baking tray with baking parchment. Rub the flour and butter together in a large bowl until the mixture resembles breadcrumbs. Stir in 25g of sugar and the mixed fruit.

Whisk the egg and milk together and stir them into the flour mixture. Stir well with a wooden spoon until the mixture comes together in a rough lump.

Place 8 spoonfuls of the mixture on the lined baking tray, spacing them well apart. Bake in the centre of the oven for 13–15 minutes or until risen and pale golden brown. Dredge with the remaining caster sugar and eat while warm.

168
CALORIES
PER CAKE

cherry bakewell tarts

MAKES 12
PREP: 20 MINUTES
COOK: 20 MINUTES

BASE
3 filo pastry sheets
(each about 45g)
oil, for brushing or spraying

TOPPING
100g reduced-sugar
jam (ideally cherry
or raspberry)
50g ground almonds
75g butter, softened
75g caster sugar
2 medium eggs, beaten
2 tbsp semi-skimmed milk
100g self-raising flour
1 tsp almond or
vanilla extract
6 glacé cherries, halved
1 tsp icing sugar, sifted,
to decorate

A filo pastry base uses very little fat and makes a crisp bottom for a light almond and cherry topping.

Preheat the oven to 200°C/Fan 180°C/Gas 6. Grease a 12-hole muffin tin with oil.

To make the base of each cake, cut each of the filo sheets into 9 evenly-sized rectangles. Make 12 stacks of 2 rectangles, lightly brushing or spraying them with oil between each layer, and arranging at opposite angles to each other.

Place a stack of filo pastry in each hole, pressing lightly into the base and sides. They don't have to be too neat, so don't be worried if the edges are crumpled. Use the remaining rectangles to patch any cracks or holes.

Stir the jam well and place a little in each pastry case.

Put the almonds, butter, sugar, eggs, milk, flour and almond or vanilla extract in a bowl and beat with a wooden spoon or an electric whisk until pale and creamy. Spoon onto the jam and then spread lightly. Dot the almond sponge with the halved cherries.

Bake the tarts for 20–25 minutes or until risen, lightly browned and firm to the touch. Leave to cool in the tin for at least 30 minutes. Sprinkle with a little sifted icing sugar to decorate. Store in an airtight tin in the fridge for up to 3 days.

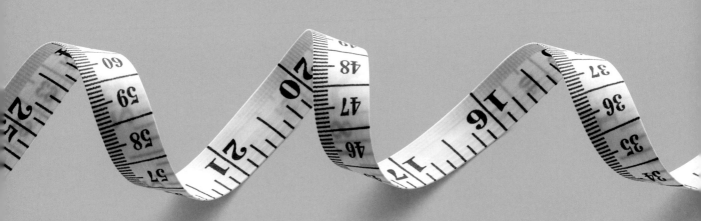

tray
bakes

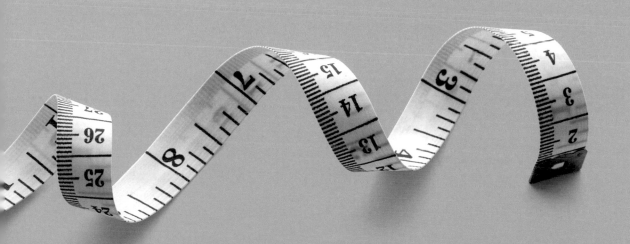

147

flapjacks

MAKES 12
PREP: 10 MINUTES
COOK: 20 MINUTES

oil, for brushing or spraying
50g butter
75g golden syrup
1 tsp vanilla extract
300g porridge oats
   (not jumbo)
3 medium egg whites

Freeze the cooked and cooled flapjack pieces in a freezer-proof container, interleaved with baking parchment, for up to 2 months. Take out as needed and defrost on a plate at room temperature for about 60 minutes before serving. For the best results, place on a baking tray in a moderate oven for 5 minutes and serve warm.

Oats are usually smothered in butter, sugar and syrup for flapjacks, but my recipe uses the minimum possible of these and still tastes sweet and satisfying. What's more, they freeze beautifully so you can just serve as many as you need.

Preheat the oven to 190°C/Fan 170°C/Gas 5. Lightly oil a 20cm loose-based square cake tin and line the base and sides with baking parchment.

Melt the butter and syrup together with the vanilla in a large non-stick saucepan over a low heat. Take the saucepan off the heat and stir in the oats until well combined.

Whisk the egg whites with a metal whisk until light and frothy. Stir into the oat mixture. Spoon the mixture into the prepared tin and press until well flattened. It's important that the oats are pressed well, so they stay firm enough to cut when baked.

Bake for 20 minutes until golden and slightly browned at the edges. Take out of the oven and mark into 12 fingers without cutting all the way through. This will make it easier to cut when cool.

Leave to cool then transfer to a board, peel off the baking parchment if necessary and carefully cut into fingers or squares with a sharp knife. Store in an airtight container, interleaved with baking parchment, for up to 3 days.

82
CALORIES
PER SERVING

chocolate brownies

MAKES 24
PREP: 15 MINUTES
COOK: 20 MINUTES

oil, for brushing or spraying
250g vacuum-packed plain
   cooked beetroot
   (not in vinegar), drained
200g self-raising flour
75g cocoa powder, sifted
1 tsp bicarbonate of soda
50g butter
50g maple syrup
50g soft light brown sugar
100ml semi-skimmed milk
2 large eggs, beaten
2 tsp icing sugar, sifted

Freeze the cooked and
cooled brownies in squares
without the icing sugar,
wrapped individually
in foil and placed in a large
freezer bag for up to
2 months. Unwrap and
defrost at room
temperature for about
1 hour before serving.
Reheat for a few seconds
in the microwave to
serve warm.

**My lower-calorie brownies are made with grated beetroot
to help keep them moist without the need for lots of butter.
Reheat for a few seconds in the microwave and serve with
low-fat custard or single cream for a comforting pudding.**

Preheat the oven to 200°C/Fan 180°C/Gas 6. Grease and line
a 20 x 30cm brownie tin (or any similar sized tin). Wearing
rubber or silicone gloves to protect your hands, coarsely grate
the beetroot and put it in a large bowl. Add the flour, cocoa and
bicarbonate of soda and toss well together until the strands
of beetroot are coated. Make a well in the centre.

Put the butter, syrup and sugar in a medium saucepan. Melt
together over a low heat, stirring regularly. Take the saucepan
off the heat and stir the milk into the hot syrup mixture, then
add the beaten eggs, stirring vigorously.

Pour the liquid slowly into the flour mixture, stirring continuously
with a wooden spoon to form a thick batter. Pour the batter
into the prepared tin. Bake in the centre of the oven for 15–18
minutes or until the cake is risen and just firm to the touch.
Serve warm or leave to cool in the tin. Dust with sifted icing
sugar and serve in small squares.

139
CALORIES
PER BAR

chewy date bars

MAKES 16
PREP: 10 MINUTES
COOK: 35 MINUTES

250g stoned soft dates,
  roughly chopped
200ml water

BASE AND TOPPING
oil, for brushing or spraying
200g plain flour
75g porridge oats
  (not jumbo oats)
50g soft light brown sugar
½ tsp baking powder
50g butter, cut into cubes
2 medium egg whites

Freeze the cooked and cooled date bars in a freezer-proof container, interleaving with baking parchment for up to 1 month. Take out the number you need and defrost at room temperature for about an hour before serving.

These sticky, crunchy, crumbly bars are low in fat and mainly sweetened with date purée. Great for a healthier lunchbox treat, you can store them in the freezer and take out just what you need.

Put the dates and water in a medium non-stick saucepan and cook over a medium heat for about 8 minutes or until thick and jammy, stirring regularly, especially towards the end of the cooking time. It doesn't matter if the date purée isn't completely smooth but it should be spreadable. If it thickens too much, simply stir in a little extra water.

Preheat the oven to 200°C/Fan 180°C/Gas 6. Grease a 20cm square loose-based cake tin and line the base and sides with baking parchment.

To make the base and topping, put the flour, oats, sugar and baking powder in a large bowl and rub in the butter until the mixture resembles coarse breadcrumbs. Lightly whisk the egg whites with a metal whisk until frothy. Stir them into the flour mixture until evenly combined.

Spread half of the flour mixture over the base of the cake tin and press down firmly to make the base of each bar. Dot with spoonfuls of the date mixture, then spread with the back of a spoon. Cover with the rest of the flour mixture and press it into the date purée. It's nice when the top is slightly crumbly and the base is firm.

Bake for 25 minutes or until lightly browned and firm. Mark into 16 squares with a sharp knife and leave to cool in the tin. Transfer to a board and cut into 16 squares. Store in an airtight tin for up to 3 days.

135
CALORIES
PER SERVING

apple strudel tray bake

SERVES 6
PREP: 15 MINUTES
COOK: 20–25 MINUTES

oil, for brushing or spraying
4 filo pastry sheets
    (each about 45g)
250g Bramley apple sauce
    (from a jar)
3 eating apples
    (each about 200g)
50g sultanas
1 tsp ground mixed spice
½ tsp ground cinnamon
1 tsp icing sugar, for
    decorating

A spiced apple filling is sandwiched between layers of filo pastry for this simple tray bake.

Preheat the oven to 200°C/Fan 180°C/Gas 6. Line a 20 x 30cm shallow baking or roasting tin. Lightly brush or spray a sheet of filo pastry with oil and place it in the tin, leaving any excess overhanging the sides. Brush or spray a second sheet of pastry with oil and place on top, then repeat with the third.

Spread the pastry with the apple sauce. Peel the apples, cut them into quarters and remove the cores. Slice the apples thinly (you'll need about 300g of sliced apple) and toss with the sultanas, mixed spice and cinnamon. Put the mixture on top of the apple sauce.

Fold in the overhanging pastry to partly cover the filling. Brush or spray the final sheet with a little oil and crumple loosely on top.

Bake for about 25 minutes or until the pastry is golden and crisp, the apples are tender and the filling is hot. (Cover with foil if the pastry is brown before the filling is ready.)

163
CALORIES
PER SERVING

banana loaf

SERVES 12
PREP: 10 MINUTES
COOK: 40 MINUTES

oil, for brushing or spraying
2 very ripe bananas (about
    225g peeled weight)
1 tsp ground mixed spice
5 tbsp sunflower oil
3 medium eggs, beaten
50g soft light brown sugar
200g self-raising flour
1 tsp baking powder
25g dried banana chips

Freeze the cooked and
cooled cake wrapped in foil
and placed in a large freezer
bag for up to 3 months.
Unwrap and defrost at room
temperature for about
3 hours before serving.
Alternatively, slice the loaf
before freezing and wrap
the individual slices in foil.
Unwrap and defrost for
about 30 minutes before
serving. Warm through
for a few seconds in the
microwave for best results.

Tip: If you don't have a food
processor, mash the bananas
with a fork and beat in
the remaining ingredients
using an electric whisk
or by hand.

Banana loaf always goes down well and it's a great way
to use up very ripe bananas that would otherwise be
thrown away.

Preheat the oven to 180°C/Fan 160°C/Gas 4. Line the base
of a 900g loaf tin with baking parchment and lightly grease
with a little oil.

Peel the bananas and cut them into short lengths. Put them
in a food processor and blend to a rough purée. Add the spice,
sunflower oil, eggs and sugar and blitz until lightly combined.
Add the flour and baking powder and blend on the pulse
setting until just combined. Don't over-blend the cake batter
or the cake will be too close textured when baked.

Pour the cake batter into the prepared tin and smooth the
surface. Top with the banana chips. Bake for 40 minutes until
a skewer inserted into the centre of the cake comes out a little
moist but clean.

Leave to cool in the tin for 5 minutes then turn out onto a wire
rack. Gently peel off the baking parchment, carefully flip the cake
the right way up and leave to cool. Cut into thin slices to serve.

easy apple tea loaf

SERVES 12
PREP: 10 MINUTES
COOK: 1¼ HOURS

3 medium eggs
2 tsp ground mixed spice
250g Bramley apple sauce
  (from a jar)
75ml sunflower oil
150g mixed dried fruit
225g self-raising flour

Freeze the cooked and cooled tea loaf wrapped in foil and placed in a freezer bag for up to 3 months. Unwrap and defrost at room temperature for about 3 hours before serving. Alternatively, slice the loaf before freezing and wrap individual slices in foil. Unwrap and defrost for about 30 minutes before serving. Warm through for a few seconds in the microwave for best results.

Using a jar of ready-made apple sauce means you don't need to add any extra sugar to this moist tea-time loaf. Just mix and bake – it really couldn't be simpler.

Preheat the oven to 180°C/Fan 160°C/Gas 4. Line the base and sides of a 900g loaf tin with baking parchment.

Use a metal whisk to beat the eggs and spice together in a large bowl. Add the apple sauce, sunflower oil and dried fruit and mix thoroughly. Stir in the flour until just combined.

Pour the cake batter into the prepared tin and smooth the surface. Bake for 1¼ hours or until the cake is well risen and lightly browned. A skewer inserted into the centre of the cake should come out clean.

Leave the cake to cool in the tin for 5 minutes then turn out onto a wire rack. Gently peel off the baking parchment and leave to cool. Cut into slices to serve.

malt loaf

SERVES 12
PREP: 10 MINUTES,
PLUS SOAKING TIME
COOK: 40 MINUTES

100ml just-boiled water
1 teabag
100g ready-to-eat
  dried prunes
4 tbsp malt extract
  (about 80g)
2 tbsp black treacle
  (about 40g)
100ml semi-skimmed milk
100g sultanas
225g self-raising flour
½ tsp baking powder
¼ tsp fine sea salt

Freeze the cooked and
cooled loaf or individual
slices wrapped in foil and
placed in a large freezer
bag for up to 3 months.
Defrost the whole loaf for
about 3 hours at room
temperature and the slices
for about 30 minutes.

Tip: You can buy malt
extract in health food stores
and online – and it lasts
for months.

Shop-bought malt loaf usually contains no added fat
and is reasonably low in calories. I've included a recipe
for a home-made malt loaf here because it's surprisingly
simple to make yet makes a pretty impressive addition
to your low-cal repertoire.

Pour the just-boiled water into a large heatproof bowl and
add the teabag. Stir a couple of times and leave to infuse
for 5 minutes. Roughly chop the prunes. Preheat the oven
to 180°C/Fan 160°C/Gas 4 and line the base and sides
of a 900g loaf tin with baking parchment.

Squeeze the teabag and discard. Stir the malt extract, treacle
and milk into the liquid until dissolved. Add the prunes and
sultanas and let it stand for 5 minutes.

Mix the flour, baking powder and salt and stir into the soaked
fruit mixture until well combined. Pour into the prepared tin
and bake for 40 minutes or until it is well risen and a skewer
inserted into the centre comes out clean. Allow to cool in the
tin then unwrap and serve in slender slices. To store, wrap
in clean baking parchment and foil. Eat within 2 days.

149
CALORIES
PER SERVING

pizza tray bake

250g white bread mix
   (from a packet)
150ml warm water
1 tbsp plain flour, for dusting
oil, for brushing or spraying
200g tomato pizza topping
   (from a jar, or see recipe,
   right)
½ yellow pepper, deseeded
   and thinly sliced
75g closed cup mushrooms,
   thinly sliced
50g pitted olives,
   drained
75g ready-grated
   mozzarella (from
   a packet)
ground black pepper

Open freeze the cooked
and cooled pizza slices
in freezer bags for up
to 1 month. Reheat from
frozen on a baking tray
in a preheated oven at
200°C/Fan 180°C/Gas 6
for 12–15 minutes or until
hot throughout.

**Home-made pizza makes a great snack or light meal when
served with a large mixed salad. This one uses a packet bread
mix and freezes well, so keep some slices handy in the freezer.**

Make the bread dough with the warm water according to the
packet instructions, kneading the dough for 5 minutes. Roll out
on a lightly floured surface into a rectangle roughly 23 x 33cm.
Lift gently and place in a lightly oiled 23 x 33cm Swiss roll tin –
or any similar-sized tin. Press the dough up the sides to fully
line the tin.

Spread the dough with the pizza topping and add the sliced
pepper, mushrooms and olives. Sprinkle with the mozzarella
and season with ground black pepper. Leave to rise at room
temperature for 1½–2 hours or until the dough is puffy and
almost double the size.

Preheat the oven to 220°C/Fan 200°C/Gas 7. Bake the pizza
for 18–20 minutes, or until it is lightly browned and the base is
cooked. Cool for 2–3minutes then cut into rectangles to serve.

Home-made tomato pizza topping: Drain a 400g can
of chopped tomatoes in a sieve for 5 minutes then tip the
tomatoes into a bowl and stir in 2 tablespoons of tomato
purée and ½ teaspoon of dried oregano. Season well with
salt and pepper. Calories per recipe: 63

192

jalapeño cornbread

SERVES 12
PREP: 15 MINUTES
COOK: 45 MINUTES

oil, for brushing or spraying
2 medium onions,
    finely chopped
250g instant (quick cook)
    polenta
25g self-raising flour
½ tsp fine salt
1 tsp baking powder
200g sweetcorn
100g drained sliced
    jalapeños (from a jar),
    roughly chopped
100g half-fat mature
    Cheddar, coarsely grated
2 large eggs
4 tbsp vegetable oil
300ml semi-skimmed milk
ground black pepper

Freeze the cooked and
cooled cornbread as
individual portions wrapped
in foil and placed in a
freezer bag for up to
3 months. For best results
reheat from frozen. Place
the wrapped portions on a
baking tray and reheat in a
preheated oven at 200°C/
Fan 180°C/Gas 6 for about
20 minutes or until hot
throughout.

A delicious, slightly spicy cornbread made with supermarket ingredients. Skinny minnies can enjoy theirs smothered in melted butter but it's just as good without. Eat just as it is with a lightly-dressed salad or with grilled meats or fish.

Preheat the oven to 200°C/Fan 180°C/Gas 6. Lightly oil a 20 x 30cm baking tin. (A small roasting or brownie tin would work well; it needs to be about 4cm deep.)

Brush or spray a large non-stick frying pan with oil and cook the chopped onions for 5 minutes over a medium-low heat or until softened and lightly coloured, stirring regularly.

Mix the polenta, flour, salt, baking powder, cooked onions, sweetcorn, jalapeños and cheese in a large bowl. Beat the eggs with the oil and milk. Season generously with ground black pepper.

Stir the liquid ingredients into the dry ingredients and beat with a wooden spoon until combined. Pour the mixture into the prepared tin and bake for 45 minutes or until golden brown and slightly risen. Serve warm in squares.

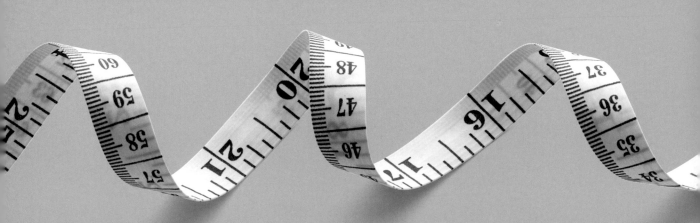

celebration
cakes

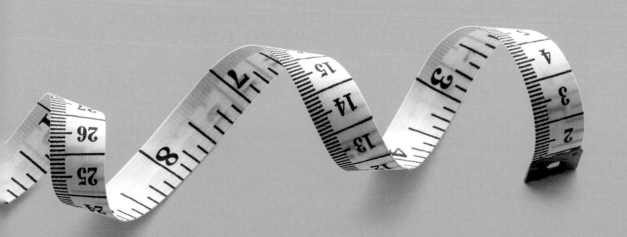

rich chocolate cake

SERVES 14
PREP: 20 MINUTES,
PLUS STANDING TIME
COOK: 35 MINUTES

oil, for brushing or spraying
2 medium eating apples
   (each about 200g)
50g butter
100g golden syrup
50g cocoa powder, sifted
100ml semi-skimmed milk
2 large eggs, beaten
150g self-raising flour
50g fresh white
   breadcrumbs
1 tsp bicarbonate of soda

DECORATION
½ tsp icing sugar

Freeze the cooked and cooled cake without decoration, wrapped in foil and placed in a freezer bag for up to 2 months. Unwrap and defrost the cake at room temperature for about 3 hours, then decorate before serving. Alternatively, reheat a slice for a few seconds in the microwave to serve warm.

This rich chocolate cake has a moist, dense texture. Serve in thin slices dusted with a little sifted icing sugar. It's also fantastic served warm in slices after reheating in the microwave for a few seconds.

Preheat the oven to 180°C/Fan 160°C/Gas 4. Grease a 21.5cm ring-shaped cake tin (large enough to hold around 1.5 litres of water) and line the base with a ring of baking parchment. Peel then coarsely grate the apples, avoiding the core (you will need 225g of grated apple) and put the grated apple in a large bowl.

Put the butter and syrup in a large non-stick saucepan. Melt them together over a low heat, stirring regularly. Add the cocoa and stir until dissolved. Take the saucepan off the heat and stir the milk into the hot syrup mixture, then add the beaten eggs, stirring vigorously.

Stir in the grated apple, then add the flour, breadcrumbs and bicarbonate of soda and stir well. Pour into the prepared tin and leave to stand for 5 minutes.

Bake the cake for 35 minutes or until it is well risen, firm to the touch and a skewer inserted into the thickest part of the cake comes out clean. Leave to cool in the tin for 10 minutes then loosen the sides by pressing lightly with your fingers all around the edge of the cake and turn it out onto a wire rack. Peel off the baking parchment and leave to cool. Dust with sifted icing sugar just before serving.

146
CALORIES
PER CUPCAKE

strawberries and cream cupcakes

MAKES 12
PREP: 25 MINUTES
COOK: 25 MINUTES

50g butter
50g golden syrup
4 tbsp semi-skimmed milk
200g self-raising flour
1 tsp bicarbonate of soda
2 medium egg yolks
1 tsp vanilla extract
2 firm but ripe pears
   (about 325g)

FROSTING
2 medium egg whites
50g caster sugar
10g cornflour (1 tbsp)
1 tsp vanilla extract
8 small fresh strawberries
   (about 75g), hulled
   and quartered

Instead of a high-fat buttercream icing, I've topped these moist vanilla sponges with a marshmallow-like reduced sugar meringue. If you don't fancy making the meringue frosting, simply dust the cakes with a teaspoon of sifted icing sugar and save 25 calories per cake.

Preheat the oven to 190°C/Fan 170°C/Gas 5. Line a 12-hole bun tin with paper fairy cake cases. Put the butter and syrup in a medium saucepan. Melt them together over a low heat, stirring regularly. Take off the heat, stir in the milk and leave to cool for 10 minutes. Put the flour and bicarbonate of soda in a large bowl and toss well together. Make a well in the centre.

Beat the egg yolks and vanilla together and add them to the butter and syrup mixture, stirring vigorously. Peel and coarsely grate the pears, avoiding the cores, (you will need about 225g grated pear) and stir them into the egg mixture.

Pour the wet ingredients gradually into the flour mixture, stirring continuously with a large metal spoon to form a thick batter. Spoon the batter into the cake cases. Bake in the centre of the oven for 18–20 minutes or until the cakes are risen and firm to the touch.

While the cakes are cooking, prepare the frosting. Whisk the egg whites with an electric whisk until stiff but not dry. Mix the sugar and cornflour and gradually whisk them into the eggs, just a teaspoon at a time, until the meringue stands in stiff peaks. Finally whisk in the vanilla.

Spoon the meringue into a large piping bag fitted with a 1.5cm star nozzle. Take the cakes out of the oven and pipe the meringue into high peaks on top. Decorate with small pieces of strawberry. Return to the oven for 4 minutes more or until the meringue is set and beginning to brown. Leave to cool in the tin. Serve the cakes the day they are made.

cheat's red velvet cake

224
CALORIES
PER SERVING

SERVES 12
PREP: 20 MINUTES
COOK: 45 MINUTES

oil, for brushing or spraying
300g vacuum-packed plain
  cooked beetroot (not
  in vinegar), drained
250g self-raising flour
50g cocoa powder, sifted
1 tsp bicarbonate of soda
50g butter
100g golden syrup
50ml semi-skimmed milk
2 large eggs, beaten

WHITE FROSTING
2 x 250g pots quark
  (fat-free soft cheese),
  drained
1 tsp vanilla bean paste
  or vanilla extract
75g icing sugar, sifted

Tip: If making ahead,
prepare the cake only,
then ice just before serving
as the beetroot colour will
leak into the quark after
a few hours.

A traditional red velvet cake is made from a chocolate sponge coloured red with food colouring, but my version uses grated beetroot for colour instead.

Preheat the oven to 180°C/Fan 160°C/Gas 4. Grease a 23cm spring-clip cake tin and line with baking parchment. Wearing rubber or silicone gloves to protect your hands, coarsely grate the beetroot and put it in a large bowl. Add the flour, cocoa and bicarbonate of soda and toss well together until the strands of beetroot are coated in the flour. Make a well in the centre.

Put the butter and syrup in a medium saucepan. Melt together over a low heat, stirring regularly. Take the saucepan off the heat and stir the milk into the hot syrup mixture, then add the beaten eggs, stirring vigorously.

Pour gradually into the flour mixture, stirring continuously with a wooden spoon to form a thick batter. Pour the batter into the prepared tin and make a slight dip in the centre with the back of a spoon to stop the cake rising too much in the centre. Bake for 45 minutes or until the cake is well risen, firm to the touch and a skewer inserted in the centre comes out clean. Leave to cool in the tin.

To make the icing, put the quark in a bowl and lightly stir in the vanilla and sugar. Turn the cake out onto a board and peel off the baking parchment. Carefully cut it in half horizontally with a large bread knife. Flip the right way up and place half of the cake on a cake stand. Spread it with a third of the frosting and cover it with the other half of the cake.

Using a palette knife in a paddling motion, spread a quarter of the remaining frosting all over the cake then chill it for 30 minutes to give the icing time to set. This should help prevent the crumbs lifting as you ice the cake. Place the reserved icing in the fridge at the same time. Take the cake out of the fridge and cover it with the remaining icing, swirling lightly with a palette knife.

167
CALORIES
PER BUN

chocolate choux buns

MAKES 8

PREP: 30 MINUTES

COOK: 40 MINUTES

oil, for brushing or spraying
50g cold butter, cut
    into cubes
125ml water
75g plain white flour, sifted
2 medium eggs, well beaten
½ tsp icing sugar,
    to decorate

CUSTARD
25g custard powder
1 tbsp caster sugar
350ml semi-skimmed milk,
    plus 1 tbsp
1 tsp vanilla extract

CHOCOLATE ICING
50g icing sugar
1 tbsp cocoa powder
2½ tsp cold water, plus a
    few drops

These choux pastry buns are generously sized but are very light. Add a low-fat custard and a drizzly chocolate icing for an impressive dessert. They will keep in the fridge for up to 2 days.

To make the custard filling, mix the custard powder and sugar with 3 tablespoons of the milk until smooth. Pour the rest of the milk (except 1 tablespoon) into a medium non-stick saucepan and stir in the custard mixture and vanilla. Heat gently, stirring continuously until the custard thickens and the sauce is smooth. Take the custard off the heat and carefully cover the surface with cling film to stop a skin forming. Leave to cool.

Preheat the oven to 200°C/Fan 180°C/Gas 6. Grease and line a large baking tray with baking parchment and set aside. To make the choux pastry, melt the butter in the water in a medium non-stick saucepan over a low heat, then bring it to the boil. Immediately tip the flour into the water and stir with a wooden spoon until the mixture forms a thick, smooth paste and leaves the sides of the pan. Remove from the heat and transfer to a mixing bowl.

Using an electric whisk, add the beaten eggs a little at a time, beating well between each addition. Spoon 8 heaps of choux paste onto the baking tray. Space them apart to allow for rising. Dip your finger in a little water and dab each peak of dough to flatten slightly. Bake for 30 minutes or until the buns are risen and golden brown.

Remove the tray from the oven and make a 5mm hole in the top of each bun by twisting the tip of a small knife or a skewer to allow the steam to escape. Return the tray to the oven for a further 10 minutes, then leave to cool.

When the custard has cooled, stir in the remaining milk and whisk until smooth and thick. Spoon into a piping bag with a 5mm plain nozzle then pipe the custard through the top of each bun.

To make the chocolate icing, sift the icing sugar and cocoa into a bowl and stir in the cold water to form a smooth pipe-able paste. Spoon into a small freezer bag. Snip a tiny corner off the bag and pipe the icing over the top of each bun. Dust with sifted icing sugar to serve.

227

mini celebration cakes

MAKES 20
PREP: 15 MINUTES,
PLUS STANDING TIME
COOK: 30 MINUTES

1 teabag
200ml just-boiled water
1 lemon
1 medium orange
300g dried mixed fruit
100g dried cranberries
3 tsp ground mixed spice
1 ripe medium banana
    (about 100g peeled
    weight)
3 large eggs, beaten
3 tbsp sunflower oil
250g self-raising flour
½ tsp baking powder

DECORATION
250g ready-made golden
    marzipan (from a packet)
2–3 tsp icing sugar,
    for dusting
250g ready-to-roll icing
    (from a packet)

Freeze the whole cake or
individually wrapped
squares, without marzipan
and icing, wrapped in foil
and placed in a freezer bag
for up to 1 month. Unwrap
and thaw the whole cake
at room temperature for
3 hours or squares for about
1 hour. Marzipan and ice the
whole cake once thawed.

**This rich fruit cake is naturally sweetened with dried fruit
and mashed banana. If you omit the marzipan and icing,
you'll save 93 calories per portion.**

Put the teabag in a measuring jug and cover with the just-boiled
water. Stir and leave to steep for 5 minutes. Finely grate the
lemon and orange zest and squeeze out the juice. Pour the juice
into a large saucepan. Squeeze the teabag and discard it. Pour
the tea into the same pan as the juice and add the lemon and
orange zest, dried mixed fruit, cranberries and spice.

Stir well and place over a low heat. Bring to a gentle simmer.
Cook very gently for 5 minutes, stirring occasionally. Remove
the saucepan from the heat, tip everything into a large mixing
bowl and leave to cool for 40 minutes or overnight.

Preheat the oven to 180°C/Fan 160°C/Gas 4. Line the base
and sides of a 20 x 30cm rectangular cake tin with baking
parchment. Peel and thickly slice the bananas into a medium
bowl. Mash to a rough purée with a fork. Add the beaten eggs
and oil and mix well. Stir in the flour and baking powder to
make a thick batter.

Spoon the batter onto the soaked fruit and stir until combined.
Spoon into the prepared tin and level the surface. Bake in the
centre of the oven for 30 minutes or until the cake is pale
golden brown and a skewer inserted into the centre comes out
clean. Remove the cake from the oven and cool it in the tin.

Carefully turn out the cake, peel off the baking parchment and
leave it to cool on a wire rack. Roll out the marzipan thinly on
a surface lightly dusted with icing sugar to a rectangle of 20 x
30cm, turning and sprinkling with a little sugar if it begins to stick.

Brush the surface of the cake with a little water. Lift the
marzipan over the rolling pin and place on the cake, pressing
down well. Do the same with the ready-rolled icing, placing it
on top of the marzipan. Trim the edges of the cake then cut it
into small squares to serve. Store in a lidded container in the
fridge for up to 5 days.

134

CALORIES
PER SERVING

strawberry cream sponge

SERVES 12
PREP: 25 MINUTES
COOK: 12 MINUTES

oil, for brushing or spraying
3 large eggs
75g caster sugar
1 tsp vanilla bean paste
  or vanilla extract
115g plain flour

FILLING
100ml whipping cream,
  chilled
100g fat-free fromage frais
75g reduced-sugar
  strawberry jam, well
  stirred to soften
250g fresh strawberries,
  hulled and halved or
  quartered if large
1 tsp icing sugar

Strawberry cream sponge is one of my favourite cakes and this lower-calorie version looks and tastes fabulous.

Preheat the oven to 200°C/Fan 180°C/Gas 6. Lightly grease and line the base of 2 x 20cm loose-based Victoria sandwich tins with baking parchment.

Put the eggs, sugar and vanilla in a large bowl and whisk using an electric whisk for 3–4 minutes or until the mixture is pale, creamy and thick enough to leave a trail when the whisk is lifted.

Sift over half the flour and use a large metal spoon to lightly fold it into the egg mixture. Sift over the remaining flour and fold it in. It's important to use gentle movements to retain as much air as possible in the batter, but you'll need to watch out for pockets of flour.

Pour the batter slowly into the prepared tins and gently spread with a spatula. Bake for 10–12 minutes until it is well risen, pale golden brown and firm to the touch. If you touch the centre of the sponge it should spring back immediately and the cakes should have begun to shrink away from the sides of the tins.

Take the cakes out of the oven and cool for 5 minutes before loosening the sides of each cake with a round-bladed knife and turning them out onto a wire rack. Gently peel off the baking parchment and leave the cakes to cool.

To make the filling, whip the cream until floppy and thick then very gently fold in the fromage frais. Put a sponge on a cake stand or plate and spread it with the softened jam.

Spoon the cream on top and spread gently. Scatter the strawberries over the cream. Gently place the other sponge on top of the fruit and dust it lightly with icing sugar. Keep in the fridge until ready to serve and eat within 2–3 days.

250
CALORIES
PER SERVING

vanilla custard slice

SERVES 8
PREP: 1 HOUR,
PLUS COOLING
COOK: 25 MINUTES

320g ready-rolled
    reduced-fat puff pastry
25g reduced-sugar
    strawberry jam

CUSTARD
25g custard powder
1 tbsp caster sugar
350ml semi-skimmed milk
1 tsp vanilla extract

WHITE ICING
100g icing sugar, sifted
5–6 tsp cold water

CHOCOLATE ICING
50g icing sugar
1 tbsp cocoa powder
2 tsp cold water, plus a
    few drops

Tip: Reduced-fat puff
pastry is available in the
chiller aisles of major
supermarkets. If using
regular puff pastry, add
an extra 20 calories
per serving.

This recipe may seem a little complicated but it is well worth the effort for such an impressive-looking pudding.

Preheat the oven to 200°C/Fan 180°C/Gas 6. Unroll the pastry onto a board and trim 3mm off the edge all the way round. Cut the pastry into 3 even rectangles, each about 11cm wide.

Place them close together on a large baking tray lined with baking parchment. Cover with a second sheet of baking parchment and place a similar-sized baking tray on top, so it completely covers the pastry. This will prevent the pastry rising too much. Bake for 15 minutes, then remove the covering tray and cook for a further 5 minutes until golden brown and leave to cool.

To make the custard, mix the custard powder and sugar with 3 tablespoons of the milk until smooth. Pour 250ml of the milk into a medium non-stick saucepan and stir in the custard mixture and vanilla. Heat gently, stirring continuously until the custard thickens. Take the saucepan off the heat, stir in the remaining cold milk and carefully cover the surface of the custard with cling film to stop a skin forming. Leave to cool.

To make the white icing, mix the icing sugar with the water until smooth and set aside. The icing should have a soft dropping consistency and not be too runny. To make the chocolate icing, sift the icing sugar and cocoa powder into a small bowl and stir in the water until smooth. Transfer to a piping or sandwich bag.

To assemble, place the pastry pieces on a board and spread the jam over two of them. Using a large spoon, dot the custard over the jam and smooth the surface. Spread the white icing over the top of the remaining pastry with a palette knife, going to the edges. Place one of the custard-covered rectangles on a platter and top with the second. Place the pastry covered with the white icing on top. Working quickly, snip off the end of the bag filled with chocolate icing and pipe lines across the white icing.

Chill the assembled dessert for 30 minutes before serving. Use a very sharp knife to cut it into 8 slices, holding each side lightly to prevent the layers separating. Eat on the same day it is made.

black bottom cakes

MAKES 12
PREP: 15 MINUTES
COOK: 20–25 MINUTES

1 eating apple (about 200g)
75g self-raising flour
40g cocoa powder, sifted
½ tsp bicarbonate of soda
25g butter
50g golden syrup
50ml semi-skimmed milk
1 large egg, beaten

CHEESECAKE FILLING
100g quark (fat-free soft
   cheese), drained
1 large egg yolk
2 tsp cornflour
1 tbsp caster sugar
1 tsp vanilla extract

Tip: Use squares of baking parchment (about 12cm squares) pressed into each hole of the cake tin instead of cake cases if you prefer. The paper will be easier to peel off than bought cases once the cakes are cooked. (You'll need to grease the tin with a little oil so the baking parchment sticks.)

American black bottom cakes are a wonderful combination of rich chocolate sponge and creamy cheesecake filling. Mine use grated apple to give a lovely, moist texture and fat-free quark for the cheesecake. You could make quark frosting (page 56) to go on top if you like, but don't forget to add an additional 18 calories to each cake.

Preheat the oven to 180°C/Fan 160°C/Gas 4. Line a 12-hole bun tin with paper cupcake cases (not muffin cases). Peel and coarsely grate the apple, avoiding the core. Mix the flour, cocoa and bicarbonate of soda in a large bowl. Make a well in the centre.

Put the butter and syrup in a medium saucepan and melt them together over a low heat, stirring regularly. Take the saucepan off the heat and stir the milk into the hot syrup mixture, then add the beaten egg, stirring vigorously. Stir in the grated apple. Pour into the dry ingredients, stirring continuously with a large metal spoon to form a thick batter. Spoon the batter into the prepared cases.

To make the cheesecake filling, use a wooden spoon to beat the quark with the egg yolk, cornflour, sugar and vanilla until smooth. Spoon the filling on top of the chocolate cake batter with a teaspoon. Bake the cakes in the centre of the oven for 20–25 minutes or until they are risen and firm to the touch. Leave them to cool in the tin.

260
CALORIES
PER SERVING

scandi salmon cheesecake

SERVES 10
PREP: 20 MINUTES
COOK: 30-35 MINUTES

oil, for brushing or spraying
500g quark (fat-free
   soft cheese), drained
250g ricotta cheese,
   drained
3 tbsp cornflour
3 large eggs
100g Jarlsberg cheese,
   coarsely grated
finely grated zest of 1 lemon
10g fresh dill, leaves
   finely chopped
15g fresh chives,
   finely chopped
flaked sea salt
ground black pepper

TOPPING
150ml soured cream
100g sliced smoked salmon
150g large cooked and
   peeled prawns, thawed
   and drained if frozen
sprigs of fresh dill and
   finely pared lemon
   zest (optional)

Tip: Cold-water prawns
have a much better flavour
than warm and are perfect
for this Scandinavian-
inspired savoury cheesecake.
Look out for prawns from
Canadian and North
Atlantic waters.

A savoury cheesecake that's proved extremely popular. It's a bit like a crustless quiche and can be served as a starter or main meal with a lightly dressed salad. If you make the cheesecake to serve 12, you will reduce the calories to 208 per serving.

Preheat the oven to 180°C/Fan 160°C/Gas 4. Lightly grease a 23cm spring-clip cake tin and line the base and sides with baking parchment.

Put the quark and ricotta cheese in a large bowl and beat lightly with an electric whisk until just combined. Gradually whisk in the cornflour, then add the eggs, one at a time, beating lightly between each addition. You may need to stop beating every now and then to push the mixture down in the bowl with a rubber spatula. The mixture should look thick, so make sure you don't over-beat it and make the cheeses too runny.

Once all the eggs have been beaten into the mixture, add the grated cheese, lemon zest, chopped dill and chives, and season with salt and lots of freshly ground black pepper.

Pour the mixture into the prepared tin. Bake for 30–35 minutes or until the cheesecake is almost set and pale golden brown. Leave to cool completely in the tin for at least an hour and then cover and chill for a further 4 hours or overnight.

When ready to serve, gently remove the cheesecake from the tin, peeling off the baking parchment if it sticks. Transfer the cheesecake carefully to a large serving plate or board.

Spoon the soured cream over the surface of the cheesecake and spread it with the back of the spoon. Tear the smoked salmon into strips and arrange them loosely on top. Scatter with the prawns and garnish with little sprigs of dill and lemon zest, if using. Serve in wedges.

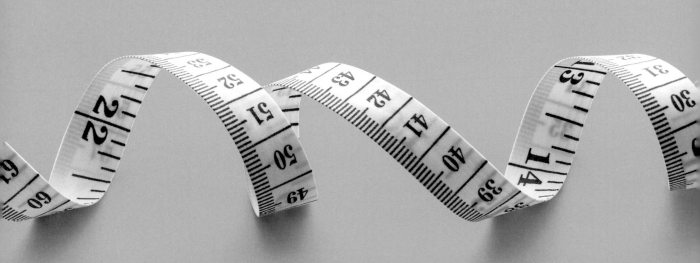

cake for pudding

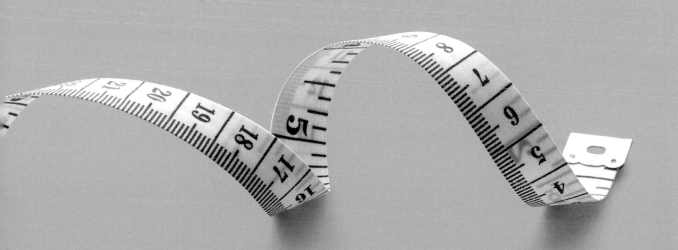

198
CALORIES
PER SERVING

dutch apple cake

SERVES 6
PREP: 25 MINUTES
COOK: 35 MINUTES

oil, for brushing or spraying
3 large eggs
100g caster sugar
finely grated zest
   of ½ lemon
1 tsp ground mixed spice
100g plain flour
500g medium cooking
   apples (about 2 medium
   apples), such as Bramley
1 tsp ground cinnamon

You will need a 2.25-litre, fairly shallow ovenproof dish for this light apple cake. A rectangular lasagne dish is ideal but a round one will work just as well.

Preheat the oven to 190°C/Fan 170°C/Gas 5. Lightly grease the base and sides of a shallow, medium-sized ovenproof dish. Put the eggs and 75g of the sugar in a large bowl and whisk using an electric whisk for 3–4 minutes or until the mixture is pale, creamy and thick enough to leave a trail when the whisk is lifted.

Mix the lemon zest and ground mixed spice together. Sift over half the flour, then use a large metal spoon to lightly fold it into the egg mixture. Sift over the remaining flour and fold in. It's important to use gentle movements to retain as much air as possible in the batter, but you'll need to watch out for pockets of flour.

Pour the cake batter into the prepared dish and put it to one side while the apples are prepared. Peel, quarter and core the apples. Cut each quarter in half again lengthwise and then slice it thinly. Don't worry if the pieces are a little uneven. Put the apples in a large bowl and toss them with the remaining 25g sugar and the cinnamon.

Scatter the spiced apples over the cake batter. Bake in the centre of the oven for 35 minutes or until well risen and golden brown. Serve warm with low-fat custard (see page 124) or single cream.

white chocolate and raspberry cheesecakes

SERVES 6
PREP: 10 MINUTES,
PLUS CHILLING TIME

65g white chocolate,
  broken into squares
100ml double cream
4 digestive biscuits
150g fresh raspberries
250g quark (fat-free soft
  cheese), drained
finely grated zest 1 lemon

Tip: Remove the chocolate from the heat before it is completely melted and let it continue to melt in the bowl, stirring occasionally with a spoon.

Quark is a naturally fat-free soft cheese and is brilliant for low-calorie desserts where you want creaminess without the calories. These little cheesecakes contain just enough chocolate to add sweetness and are full of colourful, juicy raspberries.

Melt the chocolate with the cream in a bowl over a pan of simmering water or in the microwave until smooth. Leave it to cool for 30 minutes but do not allow it to set.

Take 6 small ramekins or pretty glasses and crumble the digestive biscuits into the base of each. Roughly crush half the raspberries and divide between the dishes.

Mix the cooled melted chocolate and cream gently with the quark until smooth. Stir in the lemon zest.

Spoon the chocolate mixture gently into each glass and decorate with the remaining fresh raspberries. Cover and chill for at least 30 minutes before serving.

166
CALORIES
PER SERVING

plum and almond cake

SERVES 6
PREP: 20 MINUTES
COOK: 40-45 MINUTES

500g fresh plums, stoned
   and quartered
15g caster sugar
50ml water
oil, for brushing or spraying

SPONGE
2 large eggs
50g caster sugar
½ tsp vanilla extract
75g plain flour

25g golden marzipan
   (optional)

Tip: Check the sponge is cooked in the centre by inserting a skewer. It should come out clean or lightly coated with plum juice but not uncooked cake batter.

This cake makes a great pudding after Sunday lunch. The marzipan isn't a compulsory ingredient, but adds a lovely almond flavour to the sponge. Leave it out and you'll save about 18 calories per serving. Serve with my low-fat custard (see page 124) if you like.

Put the plums, sugar and water in a non-stick saucepan and cook over a medium heat for about 10 minutes or until softened, stirring regularly, especially towards the end of the cooking time. Take the saucepan off the heat.

Preheat the oven to 200°C/Fan 180°C/Gas 6. Lightly grease a shallow ovenproof dish – it will need to hold around 1.5 litres of liquid. To make the sponge, put the eggs, sugar and vanilla in a medium bowl and whisk using an electric whisk for 2 minutes or until the mixture is pale and thick. Sift over the flour and use a large metal spoon to lightly fold the flour into the egg mixture.

Place alternate spoonfuls of the plums and the sponge mixture into the prepared dish. Coarsely grate the marzipan, if using, and sprinkle on top. Bake for 30–35 minutes or until the sponge is well risen and pale golden brown, and the plum juice is bubbling. Serve with low-fat custard, reduced-fat cream or half-fat crème fraiche.

112
CALORIES
PER SERVING

berry jelly pots

SERVES 6

PREP: 20 MINUTES,
PLUS CHILLING TIME

COOK: 1 MINUTE

6 leaf gelatine sheets
600ml cranberry juice drink
400g mixed berries, such
  as hulled strawberries,
  raspberries, blueberries,
  redcurrants, (halve or
  quarter the strawberries
  if large)
6 sponge finger biscuits
  or madeleines

Colourful puddings with a sponge cake base, these will be popular with anyone who loves trifle. Use madeleines from the recipe on page 68 or ready-made sponge fingers. Using madeleines will add an extra 32 calories to each pot.

Put the gelatine sheets in a bowl of cold water and leave to soak for 5 minutes or until floppy. Pour the cranberry juice drink into a non-stick saucepan and heat it gently until lukewarm.

Take the gelatine sheets out of the bowl and shake off the excess water. Drop them into the warm juice and stir until dissolved. Pour into a large jug and leave to cool for 30 minutes.

Place 6 glass tumblers or dessert dishes on a small tray. Add a sponge finger or madeleine to each glass. Divide roughly half the fruit between the glasses and pour over half the liquid jelly. Place in the fridge and chill for 1½–2 hours or until the jelly is set.

Add the remaining berries and the rest of the jelly to each tumbler, cover and return to the fridge for a further 60 minutes or so until set. Eat within 2 days.

These little jellies are lovely topped with fat-free fromage frais or lightly-whipped double cream. You'll need just 75ml double cream, lightly whipped and divided between the pots. This will add 62 calories per serving. A tablespoon of fat-free fromage frais contains about 10 calories per serving.

133
CALORIES
PER SERVING

jam sponge puddings

SERVES 6
PREP: 20 MINUTES
COOK: 15-17 MINUTES

oil, for brushing or spraying
2 large eggs
50g caster sugar
1 tsp vanilla bean paste
  or vanilla extract
65g plain flour
100g reduced-sugar
  raspberry or
  strawberry jam
150g fresh or frozen
  raspberries

Open freeze the cooled sponges topped with the raspberries and jam until solid then pack in a single layer in a freezer-proof container for up to 1 month. Defrost at room temperate for about 45 minutes then reheat one at a time in the microwave for about 40 seconds. Take care as the jam will be very hot.

A lovely pudding for when the weather is cold. These sponges are topped with reduced-sugar jam and raspberries to keep the calories low. Serve with home-made low-fat custard.

Preheat the oven to 190°C/Fan 170°C/Gas 5. Lightly grease 6 individual metal pudding tins (each should hold about 175ml of liquid) or large ramekins and line the base of each with a disc of baking parchment.

Put the eggs, sugar and vanilla in a large bowl and whisk using an electric whisk for 3–4 minutes until the mixture is pale and thick enough to leave a trail when the whisk is lifted.

Sift over roughly half the flour, then use a large metal spoon to lightly fold the flour into the egg mixture. Sift over the remaining flour and fold it in. It's important to use gentle movements to retain as much air as possible in the batter, but you'll need to watch out for pockets of flour.

Spoon the batter into the prepared tins. Place the pudding basins on a baking tray and bake for 15–17 minutes or until well risen and firm to the touch. The sponge should be beginning to shrink away from the sides of the tin when they are ready.

While the sponges are cooking, place the jam and raspberries in a small non-stick saucepan and heat gently for 2–3 minutes, stirring regularly until the fruit has softened. Set aside.

Take the sponges out of the oven and cool in the tins for 5 minutes then turn out into shallow bowls. Remove the baking parchment and top with the raspberries and jam.

Low-fat custard: Mix 2 tablespoons of semi-skimmed milk with 25g of custard powder and 2 tablespoons of caster sugar. Pour 400ml of semi-skimmed milk into a medium non-stick saucepan and stir in the custard mixture and 1 teaspoon of vanilla extract. Bring to a gentle simmer over a medium heat, stirring continuously until the custard is smooth and thick. Serves 6. Calories per serving: 61

125
CALORIES
PER SERVING

chocolate amaretti cheesecake

SERVES 12
PREP: 15 MINUTES,
PLUS COOLING AND
CHILLING TIME
COOK: 25–30 MINUTES

oil, for brushing or spraying
500g quark (fat-free
    soft cheese), drained
250g ricotta cheese,
    drained
1½ tsp vanilla bean paste
    or vanilla extract
3 tbsp cornflour
3 tbsp cocoa powder, sifted
4 tbsp caster sugar
3 large eggs
30g amaretti biscuits
    (about 6)

This chocolate cheesecake isn't overly sweet or rich, so makes a welcome dessert after a large meal. It can be prepared ahead and only needs decorating with amaretti biscuits just before serving. With the added crunch of the amaretti, no one will miss the classic biscuit base.

Preheat the oven to 180°C/Fan 160°C/Gas 4. Lightly grease a 23cm spring-clip cake tin and line the base and sides with baking parchment.

Put the quark, ricotta cheese and vanilla in a large bowl and beat with an electric whisk until just combined. Mix the cornflour, sifted cocoa powder and sugar together.

Whisk the cornflour mixture into the cheeses, then add the eggs, one at a time, beating lightly between each addition. You will need to stop beating every now and then to push the mixture down the sides of the bowl with a rubber spatula. Try not to over-beat the mixture as it could become too runny.

Pour the mixture into the prepared tin. Bake for 25–30 minutes or until almost completely set. The cheesecake should still have a slight wobble in the centre. Leave to cool in the tin for at least an hour and then cover and chill for a further 3 hours or overnight.

When you are ready to serve, gently remove the cheesecake from the tin, peeling off the baking parchment if it sticks. Transfer the cheesecake carefully to a large serving plate or board. Crumble the amaretti biscuits over the top. Serve in slender wedges with extra-thick single cream if you like. Each tablespoon of single cream contains about 28 calories.

222
CALORIES
PER SERVING

lemon and blueberry cheesecake

SERVES 10

PREP: 10 MINUTES

COOK: 50 MINUTES, PLUS COOLING AND CHILLING TIME

oil, for brushing or spraying
750g ricotta cheese, drained
75g caster sugar
2 tbsp cornflour
4 large eggs
2 large egg yolks
finely grated zest of 2 lemons
1 tsp vanilla bean paste or vanilla extract

SAUCE
200g fresh blueberries
25g caster sugar
3 tbsp cold water
1 tbsp cornflour

This luscious cheesecake has a rich but light texture. The blueberry sauce complements it perfectly, but you could also top with fresh berries and a sprinkling of icing sugar.

Preheat the oven to 170°C/Fan 150°C/Gas 3½. Grease and line the base of a 23cm spring-clip cake tin with baking parchment. Place the tin on a large piece of foil and bring up the sides. This will prevent the water from getting in when baked.

To make the cheesecake, mix the sugar with the cornflour in a large bowl then add the ricotta. Using an electric beater, whisk until well combined. Gradually add the eggs and yolks, one at a time, whisking well between each addition. Stir in the lemon zest and vanilla.

Pour the cheese mixture into the prepared tin. Put the tin into a deep roasting tin and half-fill the roasting tin with just-boiled water. Carefully place the tins in the oven and bake for 50 minutes or until the cheesecake is firm with a slight wobble in the centre. If the cheesecake starts to brown while it is still very wobbly, cover the tin loosely with a large piece of foil.

Take the cheesecake out and leave it to cool in the water bath for 15 minutes. Holding the cheesecake tin with an ovencloth, take it out of the water bath and leave to cool completely. Once cool, transfer it to the fridge and chill for at least 4 hours before removing it from the tin. While the cheesecake is chilling, make the sauce. Put 100g of the blueberries, sugar and 2 tablespoons of water in a medium non-stick saucepan. Mix the remaining water with the 1 tablespoon cornflour to form a smooth paste.

Heat the blueberries gently and cook for 3–4 minutes or until they soften slightly. Stir in the cornflour mixture and cook for 1–2 minutes more or until the sauce is thickened and clear, stirring continuously. Remove from the heat and stir in the rest of the blueberries. Cover and leave to cool.

Release the cheesecake gently from the tin. Turn out onto a serving plate or cake stand and peel off any baking parchment. Spoon over the blueberry sauce and serve in slices.

fresh fruit flan

SERVES 6
PREP: 20 MINUTES
COOK: 10–12 MINUTES

oil, for brushing or spraying
2 large eggs
50g caster sugar
1 tsp vanilla extract
65g plain flour

TOPPING
150g fat-free fromage frais
1½ tsp icing sugar, sifted
1 ripe but firm peach or
   nectarine, halved, stoned,
   and sliced
250g fresh berries,
   such as strawberries,
   raspberries, blueberries
   and redcurrants

This fruit-laden flan is made in a quiche tin so it has a pretty fluted edge and is topped with fat-free fromage frais and lots of low-calorie berries.

Preheat the oven to 200°C/Fan 180°C/Gas 6. Lightly grease and line the base of a 22cm loose-based fluted quiche tin with baking parchment.

Put the eggs, sugar and vanilla in a large bowl and whisk using an electric whisk for 3 minutes or until the mixture is pale, creamy and thick enough to leave a trail when the whisk is lifted.

Sift over half the flour and use a large metal spoon to lightly fold it into the egg mixture. Sift over the remaining flour and fold it in. It's important to use gentle movements to retain as much air as possible in the batter, but you'll need to watch out for pockets of flour.

Pour the batter gently into the prepared tin and spread it with a spatula. Bake for 10–12 minutes or until well risen, pale golden brown and firm to the touch. If you touch the centre of the sponge it should spring back immediately and the cake should be beginning to shrink away from the sides of the tin.

Take the tin out of the oven and cool for 5 minutes before loosening the sides of the sponge with a round-bladed knife and turning it out onto a wire rack. Gently peel off the baking parchment and leave the flan to cool.

To make the topping, mix the fromage frais with 1 teaspoon of the icing sugar. Transfer the sponge to a plate or stand and spread the fromage frais over the centre.

If using strawberries, hull and halve or quarter them if they are large. Arrange all the fruit over the fromage frais and sift the remaining icing sugar over the top. Keep in the fridge until ready to serve and eat the same day.

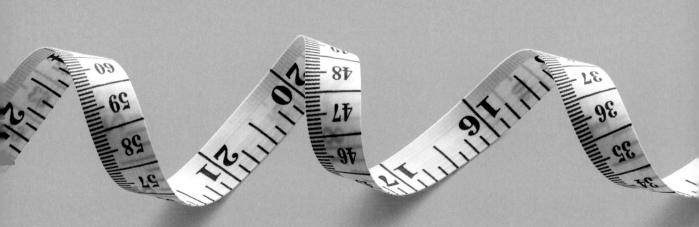

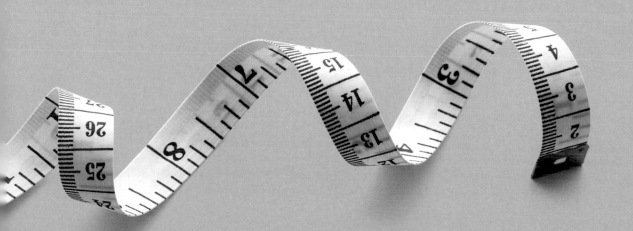

flatbread

crispbread crackers

MAKES 26
PREP: 20 MINUTES,
PLUS RISING TIME
COOK: 30 MINUTES

100ml just-boiled water
100ml cold water
7g fast-action dried yeast
1 tsp fine sea salt
200g wholemeal rye flour
125g strong white flour,
   plus extra for dusting
oil, for brushing or spraying

These rye crackers are very crisp and last for weeks in an airtight tin. Serve with deli ingredients such as smoked salmon or mackerel, hummus, salad and low-fat dips and cheeses.

Mix the just-boiled and cold water in a large bowl and whisk in the yeast and salt. Stir in both the flours and mix to form a fairly firm dough. Turn out onto a very lightly floured surface and knead for 5 minutes.

Roll out with a rolling pin until the dough is about 3mm thick. Cut into rounds with a 9cm fluted or plain biscuit cutter, re-kneading and rolling the dough until you have made 26 crispbreads. Place them on 2 large baking trays lined with baking parchment.

Cover the blunt end of a pencil or biro with cling film and punch several holes in each cracker, piercing almost all the way through. This will stop them rising too much and make them easier to break when serving. Cover loosely with oiled cling film and leave to rise in a warm place for 1 hour.

Preheat the oven to 200°C/Fan 180°C/Gas 6. Bake the crackers one tray at a time for 15 minutes or until very crisp and lightly coloured. The crackers will become crisper as they cool. Leave to cool on the trays. Pack into an airtight tin and eat within 3 weeks.

187

pitta bread

MAKES 8
PREP: 15 MINUTES,
PLUS RISING TIME
COOK: 12 MINUTES

200ml warm water
1 tsp fast-action dried yeast
1 tbsp olive oil
1 tsp caster sugar
½ tsp fine sea salt
400g strong white flour,
   plus extra for dusting
oil, for brushing or spraying

Freeze the cooked and
cooled pitta in a large
freezer bag for up to
2 months. Take out the
number you need and
defrost them at room
temperature for about
30 minutes, then toast
lightly until hot throughout
before serving.

**Pitta bread is unexpectedly simple and satisfying to make.
It should be baked in a really hot oven so it puffs up, leaving
the characteristic gap in the centre that you can fill with all
sorts of low-calorie ingredients.**

Pour the water into a large mixing bowl and stir in the yeast,
oil, sugar and salt. Add the flour and mix with a spoon and
then your hands to form a dough.

Turn the dough out onto a very lightly floured surface and
knead for 5 minutes. Place the dough in a large lightly oiled
bowl, cover and leave in a warm place for 1–1½ hours or until
it is well risen and puffy to touch.

Preheat the oven to 220°C/Fan 200°C/Gas 7. Divide the
dough into 8 equal pieces and shape them into balls. Roll out
on a lightly-floured surface into long ovals, about 5mm thick.

Place a large baking tray in the oven for 5 minutes to heat.
Working quickly but carefully, place 2 pitta breads on the tray
and bake for 4 minutes. They should rise quickly and have
a little colour.

Take the pittas off the tray with tongs and place them on a
wire rack to cool. Continue cooking the rest of the breads in
exactly the same way. Serve the breads warm or leave them
to cool before filling.

310 CALORIES PER PIZZA

easy home-made pizza

MAKES 6

PREP: 25 MINUTES,
PLUS RISING TIME

COOK: 30 MINUTES

200ml warm water
2 tsp fast-action dried yeast
1 tbsp olive oil
1 tsp caster sugar
1 tsp fine sea salt
350g strong white flour,
   plus extra for dusting
oil, for spraying or brushing

TOPPING
300g tomato pizza topping
   (from a jar or can)
100g thinly-sliced smoked
   ham, torn into strips
150g closed cup
   mushrooms, sliced
100g ready-grated
   mozzarella (from
   a packet)

ground black pepper
basil, to garnish

Open freeze the pizzas on
baking trays in the freezer
after rising. Once solid,
place in large freezer bags
and freeze for up to
1 month. Take out the
number you need and bake
the pizzas from frozen as
above for about 12 minutes.

Tip: For a veggie friendly
pizza, top with sun-blush
tomato pieces instead
of the ham.

Almost nothing beats a hot, cheesy home-made pizza, and when you've made it yourself, you can control the calories. This recipe makes six individual pizzas that can be cooked from frozen for a quick and convenient meal at short notice. It doesn't matter if your pizza bases are slightly odd shapes when you roll – in fact I think they look better for it.

Pour the water into a large mixing bowl and stir in the yeast, oil, sugar and salt. Add the flour and mix with a spoon and then your hands until the ingredients form a dough. Turn out onto a very lightly floured surface and knead for 5 minutes.

Divide the dough into 6 balls and roll each ball into a circle roughly 23cm in diameter and about 5mm thick. Place each circle on a square of baking parchment as soon as it is rolled.

Spread the pizzas with the tomato topping and arrange the ham and mushrooms over it. Sprinkle with the grated mozzarella and leave the pizzas to rise for 1–1½ hours until well risen and puffy.

Preheat the oven to 240°C/Fan 220°C/Gas 9. Spray each pizza with a little oil, or brush the edges with olive oil, and season all over with ground black pepper. Place the pizza, still on its baking parchment, on a baking tray and cook for about 5 minutes or until the cheese has melted and the edges of the pizza are golden brown.

Place on a plate and cook the other pizzas in exactly the same way. Garnish with fresh basil and eat with a large salad.

17

CALORIES
PER BREAD

italian crispbread

MAKES 20
PREP: 25 MINUTES
COOK: 15-20 MINUTES

50g '00' (pasta) flour,
   plus extra for dusting
50g semolina
½ tsp fine sea salt
5 tbsp cold water

This recipe is similar to the Italian *carta di musica* (music bread), so-called by some because it should be so thinly rolled that you can read music through it. Keeping the bread thin also means fewer calories for you. Serve with dips, low-fat soft cheeses and soups.

Mix the flour, semolina and salt in a large bowl and make a well in the centre. Slowly add the water and mix to form a soft dough. Turn the dough out onto a very lightly floured surface and knead for 10 minutes until it is smooth and elastic.

Preheat the oven to 240°C/Fan 220°C/Gas 9. Divide the dough into 20 small balls and roll out each ball in one direction to make long tongue shapes, about 20cm long and 8cm wide in the middle. They should be just 1–2mm thick. As soon as each one has been rolled, place it on a large baking sheet lined with baking parchment. You should be able to fit 4–5 'tongues' on each tray.

Bake in batches for 2½–3½ minutes or until they are puffed up and pale golden brown. Watch carefully as the crispbreads are so thin, they will be quick to burn. (If the tray is slightly warm from a previous batch, the crispbreads will take less time.)

Take them out of the oven and cool on a wire rack. The breads will continue to crisp up as they cool. Store in an airtight tin for up to 2 weeks.

72
CALORIES
PER BREAD

chapattis

MAKES 12
PREP: 20 MINUTES
COOK: 25 MINUTES

125g plain flour, plus
    extra for dusting
100g wholemeal flour
1 tsp fine sea salt
1 tbsp sunflower oil
75ml just-boiled water
75ml cold water

Freeze the uncooked
chapattis in a freezer bag
interleaved with baking
parchment for up to
1 month. Cook from frozen
as above, adding roughly
20 seconds to the time.

Chapattis make a great accompaniment to curries and are far lower in calories than naan bread or parathas. They only contain a few ingredients, so are pretty easy to knock together, and I've reduced the fat to help bring the calories down. They freeze very well, so it's worth making several at a time and then cooking them from frozen when you are ready.

Put the flours in a large bowl and stir in the salt. Rub in the sunflower oil until the dough starts to come together and feels like damp sand. Stir in the water and knead it into the dry ingredients in the bowl until the dough feels smooth and elastic.

Turn the dough onto a lightly floured surface and divide it into 12 pieces. Roll into smooth balls. Sprinkle the work surface with a little more flour and roll out a ball very thinly, using a floured rolling pin. It should be about 15cm in diameter. Turn the dough regularly and sprinkle it with a little more flour if it begins to stick. Put it to one side and continue making the rest of the chapattis in the same way.

Place a small non-stick frying pan over a high heat and once it is hot, add one of the chapattis, making sure to brush off any excess flour. Cook for about 30 seconds, then turn it over and cook it on the other side for about a minute. It should be lightly browned in patches and look fairly dry without being crisp. Press the chapatti with a spatula while cooking to encourage it to puff up and cook inside.

Put the chapatti on a plate, cover with a piece of foil and a clean tea towel to help retain the heat. Roll and cook the remaining chapattis in exactly the same way. Serve warm with yoghurt, pickles or curry.

Apple, cucumber and mint dip: Mix 300g of fat-free Greek yoghurt with 1 coarsely-grated eating apple, 1 finely chopped red chilli (optional) and 3 heaped tablespoons of chopped fresh mint leaves. Season with salt and pepper. Serves 6. Calories per serving: 33

114
CALORIES
PER WRAP

tortilla wraps

MAKES 8
PREP: 20 MINUTES,
PLUS RESTING TIME
COOK: 10 MINUTES

200g plain white flour,
   plus extra for dusting
1 tsp fine sea salt
1 tsp baking powder
50ml just-boiled water
50ml cold water
2 tbsp sunflower oil

Freeze the cooked and
cooled tortillas in a large
freezer bag, interleaved
with baking parchment,
for up to 1 month. Reheat
from frozen one at a time
in a microwave for about
15 seconds.

Making your own tortillas is quick and fun – and cheaper
than buying them. Use them for sandwich wraps or fill with
stir-fried spiced chicken, peppers and onions for a sizzling
fajita-style meal.

Put the flour, salt and baking powder in a food mixer fitted with
a dough hook and mix to lightly combine. Mix the water and
sunflower oil and add to the dry ingredients. Knead the dough
for 3 minutes until smooth and elastic. (Alternatively, mix the
water and sunflower oil into the dough and knead by hand
for 5 minutes.)

Turn the dough onto a very lightly floured surface and divide
into 8 balls. Leave them to stand for 30 minutes. Roll out each
ball with a rolling pin into roughly 20cm rounds, turning the
dough regularly so you get a nice round shape, but don't worry
if it isn't perfect. Dust flour underneath the tortillas every now
and then so they don't stick.

Place a large non-stick frying pan over a high heat until it is
very hot. Take a tortilla, brush off any excess flour and cook
for about 30 seconds on each side, pressing lightly with a
spatula as the tortilla cooks so it puffs up and brown spots form.

Turn over and cook on the other side for 20–30 seconds more
or until the tortilla is cooked but remains soft and pliable. Cook
the other tortillas in exactly the same way.

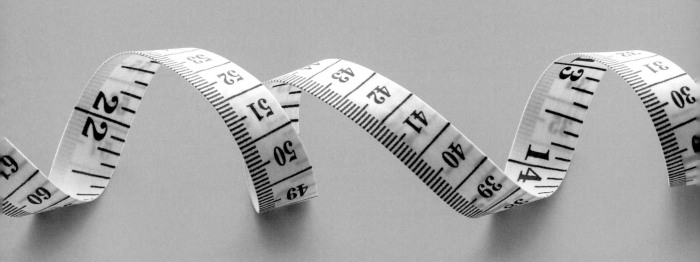

bread

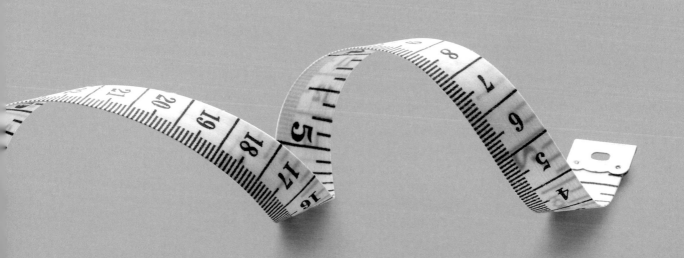

72
CALORIES
PER SLICE

very light white

**MAKES 2 LOAVES
(EACH WITH 12 SLICES)**
**PREP: 20 MINUTES,
PLUS RISING TIME**
COOK: 25 MINUTES

½ tsp fast-action
   dried yeast
150g strong white flour
150ml cold water

FOR THE FINAL DOUGH
50ml just-boiled water
100ml cold water
1 tsp fast-action dried yeast
1 tsp fine sea salt
350g strong white flour,
   plus 1 tsp extra to dust
oil, for brushing or spraying

Freeze the cooked and
cooled loaves, wrapped in
foil and placed in freezer
bags for up to 1 month.
Reheat from frozen while
still wrapped in foil at
200°C/Fan 180°C/Gas 6
for 20 minutes or until
hot throughout.

These very light and airy loaves are rather like ciabatta bread
and the dough needs to be started the day before you want to
eat them. The slices look pretty generous, but because they
are full of holes, the bread is surprisingly low in calories.
They freeze very well so keep a loaf in the freezer.

Mix the yeast and the flour in a medium bowl and stir in the
cold water with a wooden spoon to form a loose, wet dough.
Cover the bowl and leave it at room temperature for about
12 hours or overnight. This will add flavour to the bread and
help its structure.

To make the final dough, mix the just-boiled and cold water in
a large bowl and whisk in the yeast and salt. Add 350g of flour
and the dough you made previously, and mix thoroughly with
a spoon and then your hands to form a soft, sticky dough.

Turn the dough onto a very lightly floured surface and knead
by stretching the dough and folding it over itself for 10 minutes.
The dough will be sticky to begin with, but if you persevere,
it will become smoother and more elastic.

Divide the dough into 2 pieces and stretch into long blunt-
ended sausage shapes, each about 30cm. Place the dough
on two baking trays lined with baking parchment, cover with
lightly oiled cling film to stop a skin from forming, and leave to
rise for 2–3 hours or until they have more than doubled in size.

Preheat the oven to 240°C/Fan 220°C/Gas 9. Bake one tray
of bread above the other for 15 minutes then swap the trays.
Reduce the temperature to 190°C/Fan 170°C/Gas 5 and cook
for a further 10–15 minutes until the loaves are golden brown
and have a crisp crust. Leave them to cool for at least
30 minutes before slicing thinly to serve.

94
CALORIES
PER SERVING

focaccia

SERVES 12

**PREP: 15 MINUTES,
PLUS RISING TIME**

COOK: 15 MINUTES

200g strong white flour,
   plus extra for dusting
100g plain flour
7g sachet fast-action
   dried yeast
1 tsp caster sugar
1 tsp fine sea salt
100ml just-boiled water
100ml cold water
1–2 tsp olive oil, for
   brushing or spraying
1 tsp flaked sea salt
ground black pepper
1 tbsp roughly chopped
   fresh rosemary leaves,
   plus extra sprigs
   to garnish

Freeze the cooked and
cooled focaccia wrapped
tightly in foil and placed
in 1 or 2 large freezer bags.
Take the bread out of the
bag and warm up the
focaccia in the foil from
frozen in a preheated oven
at 200°C/Fan 180°C/Gas 6
for 20–25 minutes.

Tip: Use a pure olive oil
spray for the best results
and avoid any calorie-
controlled oil sprays for this
recipe as the water content
may affect the browning
of the crust.

Most focaccia is oozing with oil but I've made this version
with just enough to make the top of the bread glisten. It's still
packed with flavour from the fresh rosemary and seasoning,
so no one will feel they are missing out.

Put both the flours, the yeast, sugar and fine sea salt in a large
bowl. Mix the just-boiled and cold water and pour it onto the
flour mixture. Stir with a wooden spoon and then bring the
dough together with your hands to form a ball.

Turn the dough onto a lightly floured surface and knead for
5 minutes to make it smooth and pliable. Using a rolling pin,
roll out the dough into a long, blunt-ended oval shape, roughly
30cm long and 20cm wide. The dough should be about
1cm thick.

Lift the dough over the rolling pin onto a large, lightly-oiled
baking tray. Cover loosely with lightly-oiled cling film and
leave to rise for 1 hour until it is well risen and doubled in size.

Preheat the oven to 220°C/Fan 200°C/Gas 7. Using your index
finger, make dimples all over the dough almost all the way
through to the tin. Brush or spray the focaccia with olive oil
and sprinkle with the sea salt flakes, black pepper and chopped
rosemary. Scatter with a few tiny sprigs of rosemary.

Bake in the centre of the oven for about 15 minutes or until
it is deep golden brown. Leave to stand for 20 minutes then
cut into 12 wide slices to serve.

104

CALORIES
PER SERVING

soda bread

SERVES 14
PREP: 10 MINUTES
COOK: 35 MINUTES

300g self-raising flour
100g wholemeal flour
1 tsp bicarbonate of soda
1 tsp fine sea salt
150g pot fat-free natural
 yoghurt
150ml semi-skimmed milk

Freeze the cooked, cooled
and sliced loaf in a large
freezer bag for up to
1 month. Defrost at room
temperature for 2–3 hours
or toast slices from frozen.

**A quick and easy loaf that can be cut into about 14 slices.
Serve with hot soup or make open sandwiches. You can
also freeze the sliced loaf and toast slices from frozen.**

Preheat the oven to 220°C/Fan 200°C/Gas 7. Line a large
baking tray with baking parchment. Mix both the flours, the
bicarbonate of soda and salt in a large bowl. Make a well
in the centre.

Beat the yoghurt and milk together in a jug and pour the
mixture slowly onto the flour while stirring with a large metal
spoon or rubber spatula until the dough comes together in
a soft, squidgy mass.

Lift the dough onto the lined tray and press into a loaf shape
about 25cm long and 3cm deep. Snip the top of the loaf 5–6
times with kitchen scissors or score it deeply with a sharp
knife. Bake for 15 minutes then reduce the oven temperature
to 180°C/Fan 160°C/Gas 4 and bake for a further 20 minutes.

The bread should sound hollow when the loaf is tapped lightly
on the underside. Cool on the tray for at least 30 minutes
before serving.

leek and cheese bread

SERVES 10
PREP: 10 MINUTES
COOK: 40 MINUTES

oil, for brushing or spraying
2 large leeks, trimmed and
  cut into roughly 1cm slices
3 tbsp cold water
400g self-raising flour
1 tsp bicarbonate of soda
1 tsp fine sea salt
50g half-fat mature
  Cheddar cheese,
  coarsely grated
150g pot fat-free natural
  yoghurt
150ml semi-skimmed milk
ground black pepper

Freeze the cooked and
cooled loaf in a large freezer
bag for up to 1 month.
Defrost at room
temperature for 2–3 hours.
Warm through in a
moderate oven before
serving.

This hearty savoury loaf is packed with gently cooked leeks
and can be served with broth-style soups, salads or cold
meats. It doesn't use yeast to rise so it can be made quickly
and on the table within an hour.

Spray or brush a large non-stick frying pan with oil and place
it over a low heat. Add the sliced leeks and cook for 5 minutes
or until they are softened and lightly browned, stirring regularly
and adding a splash of water if they begin to stick. Season the
leeks with lots of ground black pepper, transfer to a plate and
leave to cool for a few minutes.

Preheat the oven to 220°C/Fan 200°C/Gas 7. Line a large
baking tray with baking parchment. Mix the flour, bicarbonate
of soda and salt in a large bowl and stir in the cooled leeks
and 25g of the cheese until evenly distributed. Make a well
in the centre.

Beat the yoghurt and milk together in a jug and pour the
mixture slowly onto the flour while stirring with a large metal
spoon or rubber spatula until the dough comes together
in a soft, squidgy mass.

Lift the dough onto the lined tray and press it into a roughly
20cm round loaf – it should be about 4cm deep. Sprinkle with
the remaining cheese. Bake for 15 minutes then reduce the oven
temperature to 180°C/Fan 160°C/Gas 4 and bake for a further
20 minutes.

The bread should sound hollow when the loaf is tapped lightly
on the underside. Cool it on the tray for at least 30 minutes
before serving.

147
CALORIES
PER MUFFIN

english muffins

MAKES 10
PREP: 20 MINUTES,
PLUS RISING TIME
COOK: 20-22 MINUTES

175ml semi-skimmed milk
1 tbsp caster sugar
10g butter
7g sachet fast-action
   dried yeast
1 medium egg, beaten
325g strong white flour,
   plus extra for dusting
1 tsp fine sea salt
1 heaped tbsp semolina

Freeze the cooked and cooled muffins in a large freezer bag for up to 2 months. Defrost them at room temperature for 1 hour before serving. Toast or warm the muffins through in a moderate oven for the best results.

Tip: If you cut the muffins in half before freezing, you can toast them from frozen.

I've made my English muffins a little smaller than the ones you buy, so the calories are lower for each serving but you won't feel you are missing out at all. They can be toasted and teamed with scrambled eggs for breakfast or filled with ham and salad for lunch, or even spread with a light scraping of butter.

Put the milk, sugar and butter in a medium saucepan and heat very gently for a few seconds until the milk is lukewarm. Take the saucepan off the heat and let the butter melt into the milk, stirring occasionally. Sprinkle the yeast over the top and whisk it into the liquid. Whisk in the beaten egg.

Mix the flour and salt in a large bowl and make a well in the centre. Pour the warm milk and egg slowly onto the flour, stirring continuously until the mixture forms a soft dough. Turn the dough onto a lightly-floured surface and knead for 10 minutes or until it is smooth, glossy and elastic. Form it into a ball, then flatten and roll out until it is about 1cm thick.

Lightly dust a large baking tray with half the semolina. Using a 7.5cm straight-sided biscuit cutter, cut out 10 muffins from the dough, re-kneading and rolling the trimmings as necessary.

Place them on the prepared tray and dust with the remaining semolina. Leave to rise at room temperature for about 1½ hours or until they are puffy to the touch and almost doubled in size.

Place a flat griddle or wide-based, non-stick frying pan over a low heat. Cook the muffins in 2 batches for 10–12 minutes, turning them every 2½ minutes until lightly browned and cooked throughout. (Use extra frying pans to save time if you have them.)

The muffins should look firm and dry at the sides. Carefully wipe the griddle or pan with a thick, dry cloth between batches so the semolina doesn't burn. Leave the muffins to stand for at least 15 minutes before serving or leave to cool then toast to serve.

no-knead bread

118 CALORIES PER SERVING

SERVES 12
PREP: 10 MINUTES,
PLUS RISING TIME
COOK: 40 MINUTES

400g strong white flour,
    plus extra for dusting
1 heaped tsp fine sea salt
½ tsp fast action dried yeast
200ml cold water
50ml just-boiled water
oil, for brushing or spraying

Freeze the cooked and cooled loaf wrapped in foil and placed in a large freezer bag for up to 1 month. Reheat from frozen wrapped in foil in a preheated oven at 200°C/Fan 180°C/Gas 6 for 30 minutes.

Tip: This loaf is cooked in a lidded casserole, which helps create steam and gives the bread a deep brown and crunchy crust.

This delicious bread doesn't need lots of stretching and pummelling, but it does require around 21 hours to rise, so make sure you start early. The resulting loaf is full of large airy holes and has a wonderfully crunchy crust. I've given an average calorie count for each slice as some will be smaller than others.

Put the flour, salt and yeast in a large bowl and stir to combine. Mix the cold and just-boiled water and stir into the flour with a large wooden spoon. Keep stirring until the mixture begins to come together and then gather it up with your fingers, pressing and turning it in the bowl for 30–60 seconds until it forms a slightly dry looking, messy ball of dough. Cover the bowl with cling film and leave the dough to rise in a warm room for 18 hours.

After 18 hours the dough should have more than doubled in size and be covered in large bubbles. Using a rubber spatula, turn the dough out onto a lightly floured surface. Working quickly but gently, lift up the sides of the dough and tuck them into the middle of the loaf until you have a nice round shape. Place a square of baking parchment roughly 30 x 30cm on a baking tray and sprinkle with 1 tablespoon flour.

Turn the dough over and place it on the floured parchment. Cover the dough with a large piece of lightly-oiled cling film to prevent a skin forming and leave to prove for a further 3 hours or until it has doubled in size.

Preheat the oven to 220°C/Fan 200°C/Gas 7. Place a lidded cast iron casserole in the oven to heat for 15 minutes. Working carefully and quickly, remove the casserole from the oven and take off the lid. Slash the surface of the dough 1–2 times with a very sharp knife and dust lightly with flour.

Gently lift the dough on the paper and lower it carefully into the hot casserole. Cover with the lid and bake in the oven for 25 minutes. Reduce the oven temperature to 200°C/Fan 180°C/Gas 6, carefully take the lid off the casserole and bake for a further 15 minutes or until the bread is golden brown and crisp. Leave it to cool on a wire rack for at least 30 minutes before slicing.

26

breadsticks

MAKES 30
PREP: 40 MINUTES,
PLUS RISING TIME
COOK: 30 MINUTES

50ml just-boiled water
50ml cold water
1½ tsp fast-action
   dried yeast
½ tsp fine sea salt
200g strong white flour,
   plus extra for dusting
1 medium egg, beaten

Tip: Sprinkle a few of your breadsticks with sesame or poppy seeds after brushing them with the beaten egg. One teaspoon of sesame seeds contains 18 calories and 1 teaspoon of poppy seeds contains 16 calories.

Home-made breadsticks keep for weeks in an airtight container and are great for serving with dips or in place of bread with soup.

Mix the just-boiled and cold water in a large mixing bowl and whisk in the yeast and salt. Add the flour and mix to form a fairly firm dough with a wooden spoon and then your hands. Turn the dough onto a very lightly floured surface and knead for 5 minutes.

Divide the dough into 30 evenly-sized pieces and roll them into very thin sausage shapes with your hands.

Place on 2 baking sheets lined with baking parchment and brush the breadsticks lightly with beaten egg. Leave to rise for 45–60 minutes or until almost doubled in size.

Preheat the oven to 240°C/Fan 220°C/Gas 9. Bake the breadsticks in 2 batches for 15 minutes or until golden brown and crisp. Leave to cool on the baking trays, then pack into airtight containers. Eat within 3 weeks.

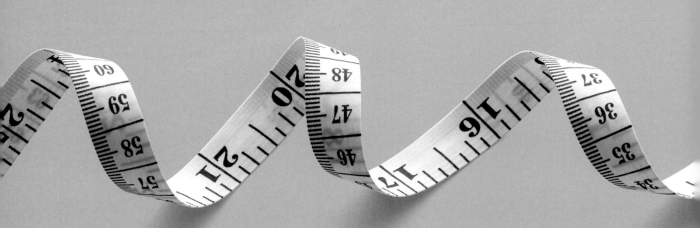

sweet
breads

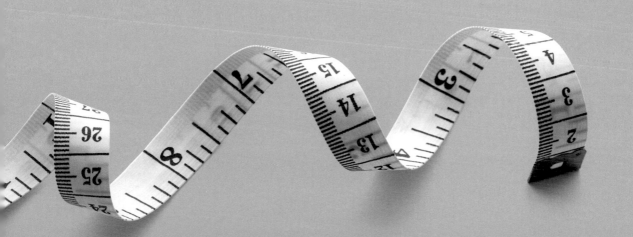

113
CALORIES
PER DOUGHNUT

baked doughnuts

MAKES 12
PREP: 25 MINUTES,
PLUS RISING TIME
COOK: 9 MINUTES

150ml semi-skimmed milk
25g butter
1 tsp fast-action dried yeast
250g self-raising flour
1 tsp baking powder
40g golden caster sugar
½ tsp fine sea salt
1 large egg, beaten
oil, for brushing or spraying

Freeze the cooked and cooled doughnuts without toppings in a large freezer bag for up to 1 month. Defrost at room temperature for about an hour then reheat for a few seconds, one at a time, in the microwave until warm before dipping them in cinnamon sugar. For best results serve warm.

Tips: If you don't have the right-sized piping bag and nozzle, put the doughnut batter in a large freezer bag and snip the end off one of the corners then pipe the batter into the tin.

If your doughnut tin only has six holes, rise and bake the doughnuts in separate batches.

Baking doughnuts rather than deep-frying them is a cinch and will help keep the calories down. Look out for ring-shaped doughnut cake tins in department stores, cook shops and online. Remember to increase the calorie count here if adding cinnamon sugar and icing.

Put the milk and butter in a small saucepan and heat very gently until the milk is lukewarm. Take the saucepan off the heat and leave to stand until the butter has melted. Whisk in the yeast.

Put the flour, baking powder, sugar and salt in a large bowl and make a well in the centre. Pour the warm milk mixture into the centre of the well, add the egg and beat hard with a wooden spoon until combined.

Transfer the batter to a large piping bag fitted with a 1.5cm plain nozzle. Carefully divide the mixture between the holes of a lightly greased non-stick doughnut tin, taking care not to overfill the holes. Leave to rise at room temperature for about an hour or until they are puffy and almost doubled in size.

Preheat the oven to 210°C/Fan 190°C/Gas 6½. Bake the doughnuts for about 9 minutes or until they are risen and golden brown. Leave to cool in the tin for 5 minutes then turn them out onto a cooling rack. Dip in cinnamon sugar or drizzle with icing (see below). Eat on the day they are made or freeze them.

Cinnamon sugar: Mix 2 tablespoons of caster sugar and ½ teaspoon of ground cinnamon in a shallow dish. Brush or spray each warm doughnut on its underside with a little cold water and dip it in the cinnamon sugar. Serve warm. Serves 12. Calories per doughnut with cinnamon sugar: 119

Icing: Mix 50g of icing sugar with 2 teaspoons of cold water until smooth. Colour with a little food colouring paste if you like. Drizzle over the cooled doughnuts, sprinkle with 10g of hundreds and thousands and leave to set for about 30 minutes before serving. Serves 12. Calories per doughnut with icing: 132

lightly-fruited teacakes

MAKES 10
PREP: 15 MINUTES,
PLUS RISING TIME
COOK: 12–15 MINUTES

175ml semi-skimmed milk,
    plus 2 tsp for glazing
40g butter, cubed
40g caster sugar
7g sachet fast-action
    dried yeast
1 large egg, beaten
375g strong white flour,
    plus extra for dusting
½ tsp fine sea salt
1 tsp ground mixed spice
finely grated zest of 1 lemon
65g mixed dried fruit
oil, for brushing or spraying

Freeze the cooked and
cooled teacakes, cut in half
and put back together in
a large freezer bag for up
to 2 months. Toast from
frozen until hot and lightly
browned. Alternatively,
freeze whole and defrost
at room temperature for
1 hour before toasting.

These teacakes are large, flattish buns, made with just a little sugar and butter and a smattering of dried fruit. They taste like a real treat but are lower in calories than the traditional kind.

Put the milk, butter and sugar in a small saucepan and heat until the milk is lukewarm. Take the saucepan off the heat and leave to stand until the butter melts. Whisk in the yeast and then the beaten egg.

Mix the flour, salt, spice and lemon zest in a large bowl and make a well in the centre. Stir in the warm milk mixture and mix to form a dough. Turn onto a very lightly floured surface and knead for 10 minutes. Knead the dried fruit into the dough.

Divide the dough into 10 pieces. Roll each piece into a ball then pull the dough from around the sides to underneath each bun to give it a neat shape. Take a ball and flatten it in your hands to make a round roughly 10cm in diameter.

Place the buns on 2 baking trays lined with baking parchment. Cover loosely with lightly-oiled cling film and leave to rise at room temperature for 1½ hours or until the buns are puffed up and almost doubled in size.

Preheat the oven to 190°C/Fan 170°C/Gas 5. Remove the cling film and brush the buns with a little milk. Bake for 12–15 minutes or until risen and golden brown. Serve the teacakes warm or leave to cool then cut in half and toast.

185 CALORIES PER CAKE

orange babas

MAKES 6
PREP: 20 MINUTES, PLUS RISING AND CHILLING TIME
COOK: 13–15 MINUTES

oil, for brushing or spraying
115g plain flour
2 tsp fast-action dried yeast
finely grated zest of
   1 medium orange
finely grated zest of 1 lemon
1/4 tsp fine sea salt
2 large eggs, beaten
2 tbsp semi-skimmed milk
25g butter, well softened
   but not melted

ORANGE SAUCE
400ml orange juice
   (from a carton)
4 tbsp orange liqueur,
   such as Cointreau

Tip: The baba batter will reach the top of the muffin tins, which is why it is important to place the tin inside a deep roasting tin for rising before covering with the cling film. I used a heart-shaped muffin tray for the babas in the photograph.

Rather than lots of rum and a sugary syrup, my orange babas are soaked in a light sauce made from orange juice and just a touch of orange liqueur.

Oil a deep 6-hole muffin tin and set it on a baking tray (use a silicone muffin tray if you like). Sift the flour into a large bowl and stir in the yeast, orange and lemon zest and salt. Whisk the eggs and milk together. Beat the egg mixture and softened butter into the dry ingredients with a wooden spoon for about 5 minutes or until very smooth and glossy.

Spoon the mixture into the prepared tin and place it in a deep roasting tin. Cover the roasting tin loosely with oiled cling film and put the babas in a warm place to rise for 1–1½ hours or until almost doubled in size. Preheat the oven to 190°C/Fan 170°C/Gas 5. Take the muffin tin out of the roasting tin and bake the babas for 13–15 minutes or until well risen and golden brown.

While the babas are baking, make the orange sauce. Put the orange juice in a wide-based frying pan. Bring to the boil, then reduce the heat slightly and simmer for 3–5 minutes or until the liquid is reduced to about 350ml. Remove from the heat and stir in the orange liqueur.

Remove the babas from the oven and cool in the tin for 5 minutes. Loosen the sides with a blunt-ended knife and place the babas in the frying pan with the sauce. Turn the babas in the sauce a couple of times then leave them to stand for 30 minutes, turning them every 10 minutes as they soak up the orange sauce.

Transfer the babas and any remaining sauce to a serving dish. Cover and chill in the fridge for at least 2 hours before serving. Serve a baba per person with a little orange sauce and some single cream (add an extra 29 calories per serving) or fat-free Greek yoghurt (add an extra 10 calories per serving).

giant crumpet

SERVES 8
**PREP: 15–16 MINUTES,
PLUS RISING TIME**
COOK: 20 MINUTES

200ml semi-skimmed milk
100g strong white flour
100g plain flour
7g sachet fast-action
   dried yeast
½ tsp fine sea salt
1 tsp caster sugar
oil, for brushing or spraying
1 tsp bicarbonate of soda
75ml warm water

Freeze wedges of the
cooked and cooled crumpet
flat in small freezer bags.
Defrost at room temperature
for 30 minutes, then reheat
the crumpet in the
microwave or toast until hot.

Tip: You may find that your
batter thickens and the
bubbles do not burst. If this
occurs, simply prick the
bubbles with a cocktail stick
as they rise to the surface.

**Making individual crumpets is a time-consuming process,
so I make a giant one instead. Cut into wedges and served
warm with just a smear of butter, it has a wonderfully
crunchy bottom and a light and airy top.**

Put the milk in a saucepan and warm very gently until tepid.
Sift the flours into a large bowl and stir in the yeast, salt and
sugar. Make a well in the centre and stir in the warm milk. Beat
well with a wooden spoon for about 3 minutes or until the
batter is thick and elastic. Cover the bowl and leave the batter
to rise in a warm place for an hour or until it has doubled
in size.

Oil a medium non-stick frying pan about 20cm in diameter.
Mix the bicarbonate of soda with the warm water. Beat it into
the batter until smooth then pour the batter into the prepared
frying pan and spread it to the sides. Leave to prove for a
further 30–45 minutes. By this time the batter should look
risen and be covered with tiny bubbles.

Place the pan over a low heat and cook for 12 minutes or until
lots of tiny bubbles have risen to the surface and burst (see tip,
left) and the top looks dry and set and is shrinking away from
the sides of the pan. (Keep the heat low or the crumpet could
burn on the bottom.)

Carefully flip the crumpet over onto a plate, then return it
to the pan and cook on the other side for about 6–8 minutes
or until it is lightly browned. Transfer to a board, spread with
a little butter if you like (add an extra 35 calories per teaspoon
of butter) and serve in wedges.

147
CALORIES
PER ROLL

chocolate breakfast rolls

MAKES 8
PREP: 25 MINUTES,
PLUS PROVING TIME
COOK: 12–15 MINUTES

250g white bread mix
 (from a packet)
25g caster sugar
100ml just-boiled water
50ml semi-skimmed milk,
 plus 2 tsp for glazing
1 tbsp plain flour, for dusting
45g plain chocolate, broken
 into 8 squares (about
 50% cocoa solids)

Freeze the cooked and cooled rolls wrapped individually in foil in a large freezer bag for up to 1 month. Reheat from frozen on a baking tray in a preheated oven at 200°C/Fan 180°C/Gas 6 for 20 minutes then remove the foil before serving.

Pain au chocolat and chocolate croissants are one of my favourite breakfasts but they are hideously high in calories, so when I'm trying to lose a few pounds, I revert to these delicious rolls for my morning chocolate fix.

Put the bread mix in a large bowl and add the sugar. Mix the water with the milk and stir into the bread mix to form a soft dough. Turn the dough onto a lightly floured surface and knead for 5 minutes.

Divide the dough into 8 pieces and roll each one into a ball, pulling the sides up and tucking the ends into the centre to create a neat shape. Take one of the balls and flatten it in your hand to make a round roughly 6cm in diameter. Add a square of chocolate, placing it in the centre of the round.

Bring up the sides of the dough to enclose the chocolate and pinch very firmly to seal the dough into a purse shape. Turn the dough over and roll it between your palms into a long, oval, egg-sized ball. (It's important that there aren't any cracks in the dough or the chocolate could seep out as the rolls are baking.)

Place the rolls on a baking tray lined with baking parchment. Brush each roll with a little milk and leave to rise for 1 hour or until doubled in size.

Preheat the oven to 200°C/Fan 180°C/Gas 6. Bake the rolls for 12–15 minutes, or until lightly browned and cooked through. Leave them to cool on the tray for 5–10 minutes before serving as the chocolate will be extremely hot.

108
CALORIES
PER BUN

easy iced buns

MAKES 12
PREP: 20 MINUTES,
PLUS PROVING TIME
COOK: 15 MINUTES

250g white bread mix
(from a packet)
25g caster sugar
100ml semi-skimmed milk
100ml just-boiled water
2 tbsp plain flour,
for dusting

FILLING AND ICING
80g reduced-sugar
raspberry jam
50g icing sugar, sifted
2 tsp cold water
food colouring paste
(optional)

Freeze the cooked and cooled filled buns without the icing in a large freezer bag for up to 1 month. Thaw at room temperature for 1 hour then top with the icing or dusted icing sugar if you prefer.

Tip: A white bread mix is easy to use, works beautifully and has just the right texture.

I love iced finger buns and can't resist them when I see them in the bakery or supermarket. These ones are a little smaller than most shop-bought versions and I've used reduced-sugar jam and just a drizzle of icing to help keep the calories low.

Put the bread mix in a large bowl and add the sugar. Put 1 tablespoon of the milk in a small bowl to glaze the buns. Mix the water with the remaining milk and stir them into the bread mix to form a soft dough. Turn the dough onto a floured surface and knead for 10 minutes. The dough will feel fairly wet, but you should not need to add extra flour.

Divide the dough into 12 pieces and roll each into a ball, pulling the sides up and tucking the ends into the centre to create a neat shape. Turn them over and roll into sausage shapes roughly the length of your middle finger (about 10cm long).

Place the buns on a baking tray lined with baking parchment just 2cm apart so they touch as they rise. Brush each bun with a little milk and leave to rise for 1 hour or until doubled in size.

Preheat the oven to 200°C/Fan 180°C/Gas 6. Bake the buns for about 15 minutes, or until lightly browned and cooked through. Leave to cool. Make the icing by mixing the icing sugar and water in a bowl until smooth (add a little more water if needed). Stir in a little food colouring paste if you like. Transfer to a small plastic freezer bag.

Make a hole with a skewer in one end of each bun and running almost all the way through to the other end. Put the jam in a piping bag fitted with a 5mm plain nozzle and pipe the jam into each bun. Place the buns on a cooling rack set over a tray.

Snip a tiny piece off a corner of the freezer bag holding the icing and drizzle the buns with the icing. Leave for 30 minutes until the icing is softly set before serving.

Lemon iced buns: Fill the buns with lemon curd instead of reduced-sugar jam and mix the icing sugar with lemon juice instead of water. Add some food colouring paste if you like. Makes 12. Calories per bun: 123

a few notes on the recipes

INGREDIENTS

Where possible, choose free-range chicken, meat and eggs. I generally use white flour, but you can try adding a proportion of wholemeal flour to the recipes. Be aware that you may need extra liquid to compensate.

Unless otherwise stated, the recipes use white sugar as it is easier to get hold of, but you can use golden caster sugar if you prefer. Maple syrup and honey can be used instead of sugar in recipes where it is used for a touch of sweetness, usually less than 50g, but not in whisked sponge recipes where it is needed to add body to the final cake.

PREPARATION

Do as much preparation as possible before you start to cook. Discard any damaged bits, and wipe or wash fresh produce before preparation unless it's going to be peeled.

Onions, garlic and shallots are peeled unless otherwise stated, and vegetables are trimmed. Lemons, limes and oranges should be well washed before the zest is grated. Weigh fresh herbs in a bunch, then trim off the stalks before chopping the leaves. I've used medium-sized vegetables unless stated. As a rule of thumb, a medium-sized onion and potato (such as Maris Piper) weighs about 150g.

All chopped and sliced meat, poultry, fish and vegetable sizes are approximate. Don't worry if your pieces are a bit larger or smaller than indicated, but try to keep to roughly the size so the cooking times are accurate. Even-sized pieces will cook at the same rate, which is especially important for meat and fish.

I love using fresh herbs in my recipes, but you can substitute frozen herbs in most cases. Dried herbs will give a different, more intense flavour, so use them sparingly.

The recipes have been tested using sunflower oil, but you can substitute vegetable, rapeseed or mild olive oil.

CALORIE COUNTS

Nutritional information does not include the optional serving suggestions. When shopping, you may see calories described as kilocalories on food labels; they are the same thing.

HOW TO FREEZE

Freezing food will save you time and money, and lots of the recipes in this book freeze extremely well. If you don't need all the servings at the same time, freeze the rest for another day. Where there are no instructions for freezing a dish, freezing won't give the best results once reheated.

When freezing food, it's important to cool it rapidly after cooking. Separate what you want to freeze from what you're going to serve and place in shallow, freezer-proof containers or freezer bags. The shallower the container, the quicker the food will cool (putting it in the freezer while it's still warm will raise the freezer temperature and could affect other foods). Cover loosely, then freeze as soon as it's cool. You can cool food more rapidly by placing the container in a sink of iced water, stirring and replacing the ice regularly. I try to get everything I want to freeze in the freezer within an hour. For baked recipes, cool on a wire rack and freeze the day it is made.

If you're freezing a lot of food at once, for example after a bulk cooking session or a big shop, flip the fast freeze button on at least two hours before adding the new dishes and leave it on for twenty-four hours afterwards. This will reduce the temperature of your freezer and help ensure that food is frozen as rapidly as possible.

When freezing food, expel as much air as possible by wrapping it tightly in good quality cling film, a freezer bag or foil to help prevent icy patches, freezer burn and discolouration, or flavour transfer between dishes. Liquids expand when frozen, so leave a 4–5cm gap at the top of containers.

If you have a small freezer and need to save space, flat-freeze thick soups, sauces and casseroles in strong zip-seal freezer bags. Fill the bag halfway, then turn it over and flatten it until it is around 1–2cm thick, pressing out as much air as possible and sealing firmly. Place on a baking tray and freeze. Once solid, the baking tray can be removed and the bags stacked.

Place delicate foods such as fresh berries, butter iced cakes and sliced cakes on a tray lined with baking parchment, and freeze in a single layer until solid before placing in containers or freezer bags. This method is called open freezing and helps stop foods sticking together in a block, so you can grab what you need easily.

Label everything clearly, and add the date so you know when to eat it at its best. I aim to use food from the freezer within about four months.

DEFROSTING

For the best results, most foods should be defrosted slowly in the fridge for several hours or overnight. For safety's sake, do not thaw dishes at room temperature. (Unless thawing un-iced cakes, biscuits and breads that would normally be stored out of the fridge.)

Flat-frozen foods (see page 177) will thaw and begin to reheat at almost the same time. Just rinse the bag under hot water and break the mixture into a wide-based pan. Add a dash of water and warm over a low heat until thawed. Increase the heat, adding a little more water if necessary, and simmer until piping hot throughout.

Ensure that any foods that have been frozen are thoroughly cooked or reheated before serving.

HOW TO GET THE BEST RESULTS

Measuring with spoons

Spoon measurements are level unless otherwise stated. Use a set of measuring spoons for the best results; they're endlessly useful, especially if you're watching your sugar, salt or fat intake.

> 1 tsp (1 teaspoon) = 5ml
> 1 dsp (1 dessertspoon) = 10ml
> 1 tbsp (1 tablespoon) = 15ml

A scant measure is just below level and a heaped measure is just above. An Australian tablespoon holds 20ml, so Australian cooks should use 3 level teaspoon measures instead.

CONVERSION CHARTS

Oven temperature guide

	Electricity °C	Electricity °F	Electricity (fan) °C	Gas Mark
Very cool	110	225	90	$^1/_4$
	120	250	100	$^1/_2$
Cool	140	275	120	1
	150	300	130	2
Moderate	160	325	140	3
	170	350	160	4
Moderately hot	190	375	170	5
	200	400	180	6
Hot	220	425	200	7
	230	450	210	8
Very hot	240	475	220	9

Liquid measurements

Metric	Imperial	Australian	US
25ml	1fl oz		
60ml	2fl oz	$^1/_4$ cup	$^1/_4$ cup
75ml	3fl oz		
100ml	3$^1/_2$fl oz		
120ml	4fl oz	$^1/_2$ cup	$^1/_2$ cup
150ml	5fl oz		
180ml	6fl oz	$^3/_4$ cup	$^3/_4$ cup
200ml	7fl oz		
250ml	9fl oz	1 cup	1 cup
300ml	10$^1/_2$fl oz	1$^1/_4$ cups	1$^1/_4$ cups
350ml	12$^1/_2$fl oz	1$^1/_2$ cups	1$^1/_2$ cups
400ml	14fl oz	1$^3/_4$ cups	1$^3/_4$ cups
450ml	16fl oz	2 cups	2 cups
600ml	1 pint	2$^1/_2$ cups	2$^1/_2$ cups
750ml	1$^1/_4$ pints	3 cups	3 cups
900ml	1$^1/_2$ pints	3$^1/_2$ cups	3$^1/_2$ cups
1 litre	1$^3/_4$ pints	1 quart or 4 cups	1 quart or 4 cups
1.2 litres	2 pints		
1.4 litres	2$^1/_2$ pints		
1.5 litres	2$^3/_4$ pints		
1.7 litres	3 pints		
2 litres	3$^1/_2$ pints		

occasional extras

No time to bake? Try these healthier snacks instead. As tempting as baked goodies are, it's much better to reduce the amount you eat or cut them out all together when you want to lose weight and keep it off. See page 6 for more information on occasional extras and how they fit into the 123 Plan.

100g strawberries, 27 cals

1 small pear (about 115g), 41 cals

100g seedless green grapes, 60 cals

60g hummus, 112 cals

small can tuna in brine – (80g can, 56g drained weight), 55 cals

75g raspberries, 19 cals

30g pitted green olives in brine, 31 cals

2 rye crispbreds, 62 cals

50g smoked salmon, 71 cals

50g sliced cooked ham, 54 cals

30g dried apricots, 56 cals

25g raisins, 68 cals

75g blueberries, 41 cals

1 orange (about 230g), 60 cals

1 small banana (about 155g), 96 cals

2 clementines, 44 cals

1 large hard-boiled egg, 80 cals

25g mixed nuts (cashews, walnuts, almonds, pecan and hazlenuts), 145 cals

½ medium avocado, 150 cals

1 round rice cake, 30 cals

1 small apple (about 130g), 55 cals

2 Jaffa Cakes, 92 cals

100g peeled carrot sticks, 35 cals

20g piece of mature cheddar cheese, 83 cals

100g skinless cooked chicken breast (roasted), 153 cals

75g cherry tomatoes, 14 cals

nutritional information
per serving

page 10 / makes 16
oaty raisin cookies

104 energy (kcal)
440 energy (kJ)
2.1 protein (g)
17.9 carbohydrate (g)
3.1 fat (g)
1.7 saturated fat (g)
1.0 fibre (g)
5.6 sugars (g)

page 12 / makes 20
iced rings

56/26* energy (kcal)
235/112* energy (kJ)
0.9/0.5* protein (g)
10.8/4.2* carb (g)
1.3/0.9* fat (g)
0.8/0.6* sat fat (g)
0.3/0.2* fibre (g)
5.0/1.4* sugars (g)
*chocolate pennies

page 14 / makes 16
coconut cookies

93 energy (kcal)
390 energy (kJ)
1.8 protein (g)
11.0 carbohydrate (g)
4.9 fat (g)
3.4 saturated fat (g)
1.2 fibre (g)
2.0 sugars (g)

page 16 / makes 20
chocolate chip biscuits

66 energy (kcal)
277 energy (kJ)
1.8 protein (g)
11.8 carbohydrate (g)
1.5 fat (g)
0.8 saturated fat (g)
0.6 fibre (g)
5.6 sugars (g)

page 18 / makes 20
lemon and white chocolate biscuits

62 energy (kcal)
261 energy (kJ)
1.6 protein (g)
12.6 carbohydrate (g)
0.9 fat (g)
0.4 saturated fat (g)
0.5 fibre (g)
5.5 sugars (g)

page 20 / makes 24
ginger snaps

31 energy (kcal)
133 energy (kJ)
0.8 protein (g)
6.8 carbohydrate (g)
0.4 fat (g)
0.1 saturated fat (g)
0.2 fibre (g)
2.2 sugars (g)

page 22 / makes 32
white chocolate and cranberry cookies

58 energy (kcal)
243 energy (kJ)
1.1 protein (g)
9.3 carbohydrate (g)
2.0 fat (g)
1.1 saturated fat (g)
0.5 fibre (g)
3.0 sugars (g)

page 24 / makes 32
maryland-style cookies

60 energy (kcal)
251 energy (kJ)
1.1 protein (g)
8.7 carbohydrate (g)
2.5 fat (g)
1.1 saturated fat (g)
0.6 fibre (g)
2.5 sugars (g)

page 26 / makes 8
chocolate rice cakes

55 energy (kcal)
232 energy (kJ)
1.0 protein (g)
9.7 carbohydrate (g)
1.7 fat (g)
0.9 saturated fat (g)
0.6 fibre (g)
3.3 sugars (g)

page 28 / makes 40
oatcake thins

25 energy (kcal)
106 energy (kJ)
0.6 protein (g)
4.0 carbohydrate (g)
0.9 fat (g)
0.3 saturated fat (g)
0.4 fibre (g)

page 30 / makes 24
savoury spiced biscuits

46 energy (kcal)
194 energy (kJ)
1.2 protein (g)
5.9 carbohydrate (g)
2.1 fat (g)
1.2 saturated fat (g)
0.7 fibre (g)
0.2 sugars (g)

page 34 / makes 12
mixed berry muffins

150 energy (kcal)
632 energy (kJ)
4.2 protein (g)
24.3 carbohydrate (g)
4.6 fat (g)
0.9 saturated fat (g)
1.5 fibre (g)
6.8 sugars (g)

page 36 / makes 12
lemon drizzle muffins

144/33* energy (kcal)
610/141* energy (kJ)
3.8/0* protein (g)
23.5/8.8 carb (g)
4.6/0* fat (g)
0.8/0* saturated fat (g)
1.0/0* fibre (g)
6.3/8.7* sugars (g)
*runny lemon icing

page 38 / makes 12
chocolate chip muffins

170 energy (kcal)
719 energy (kJ)
5.2 protein (g)
25.4 carbohydrate (g)
6.1 fat (g)
1.8 saturated fat (g)
2.2 fibre (g)
9.1 sugars (g)

page 40 / makes 12
apple and raisin muffins

157 energy (kcal)
665 energy (kJ)
4.3 protein (g)
26.3 carbohydrate (g)
4.7 fat (g)
0.9 saturated fat (g)
1.4 fibre (g)
9.1 sugars (g)

page 42 / makes 12
breakfast muffins

172 energy (kcal)
724 energy (kJ)
4.9 protein (g)
27.6 carbohydrate (g)
5.4 fat (g)
1.0 saturated fat (g)
2.1 fibre (g)
8.7 sugars (g)

page 44 / makes 6
raspberry scones

219 energy (kcal)
923 energy (kJ)
4.8 protein (g)
36.2 carbohydrate (g)
7.1 fat (g)
4.2 saturated fat (g)
2.2 fibre (g)
4.0 sugars (g)

page 46 / serves 4
potato scones

135 energy (kcal)
566 energy (kJ)
2.4 protein (g)
20.3 carbohydrate (g)
5.4 fat (g)
3.3 saturated fat (g)
1.6 fibre (g)
0.6 sugars (g)

page 50 / makes 12
chocolate crispy cakes

27 energy (kcal)
112 energy (kJ)
0.4 protein (g)
5.2 carbohydrate (g)
0.6 fat (g)
0.4 saturated fat (g)
0.1 fibre (g)
1.7 sugars (g)

page 52 / serves 12
carrot cake with soft cheese frosting

167 energy (kcal)
702 energy (kJ)
6.9 protein (g)
24.4 carbohydrate (g)
5.3 fat (g)
2.7 saturated fat (g)
1.7 fibre (g)
8.8 sugars (g)

page 54 / serves 16
coffee maple pecan cake

160 energy (kcal)
647 energy (kJ)
3.4 protein (g)
25.4 carbohydrate (g)
5.6 fat (g)
0.9 saturated fat (g)
1.9 fibre (g)
11.9 sugars (g)

page 56 / makes 12
caramel cakes with vanilla frosting

136/49* energy (kcal)
571/208* energy (kJ)
4.6/7.7* protein (g)
19.9/4.6* carb (g)
4.7/0.1* fat (g)
2.5/0.1* sat fat (g)
1.1/0* fibre (g)
7.5/4.4* sugars (g)
*home-made quark

page 58 / makes 12
little banoffee cakes

161 energy (kcal)
679 energy (kJ)
3.0 protein (g)
26.2 carbohydrate (g)
5.6 fat (g)
2.7 saturated fat (g)
0.9 fibre (g)
14.3 sugars (g)

page 60 / serves 12
ginger cake with lime icing

188 energy (kcal)
794 energy (kJ)
4.0 protein (g)
32.9 carbohydrate (g)
5.3 fat (g)
2.7 saturated fat (g)
1.1 fibre (g)
17.3 sugars (g)

page 62 / makes 12
little eccles cakes

123 energy (kcal)
518 energy (kJ)
2.2 protein (g)
17.8 carbohydrate (g)
5.1 fat (g)
2.6 saturated fat (g)
0.4 fibre (g)
6.9 sugars (g)

page 64 / serves 8
strawberry jam swiss roll

142 energy (kcal)
600 energy (kJ)
4.4 protein (g)
25.3 carbohydrate (g)
3.2 fat (g)
0.9 saturated fat (g)
0.7 fibre (g)
15.8 sugars (g)

page 66 / serves 8
double chocolate swiss roll

154 energy (kcal)
648 energy (kJ)
4.7 protein (g)
24.6 carbohydrate (g)
4.7 fat (g)
1.7 saturated fat (g)
0.9 fibre (g)
17.2 sugars (g)

page 68 / makes 12
madeleines

56 energy (kcal)
236 energy (kJ)
2.0 protein (g)
9.2 carbohydrate (g)
1.5 fat (g)
0.4 saturated fat (g)
0.3 fibre (g)
4.5 sugars (g)

page 70 / makes 8
mary's rock cakes

172 energy (kcal)
724 energy (kJ)
3.4 protein (g)
27 carbohydrate (g)
6.3 fat (g)
3.6 saturated fat (g)
1.2 fibre (g)
8.4 sugars (g)

page 72 / makes 12
cherry bakewell tarts

168 energy (kcal)
705 energy (kJ)
3.3 protein (g)
19.8 carbohydrate (g)
8.9 fat (g)
3.8 saturated fat (g)
0.5 fibre (g)
11.5 sugars (g)

page 76 / makes 12
flap jack

147 energy (kcal)
613 energy (kJ)
3.4 protein (g)
20 carbohydrate (g)
5.5 fat (g)
2.6 saturated fat (g)
2.2 fibre (g)
5.2 sugars (g)

page 78 / makes 24
chocolate brownies

82 energy (kcal)
344 energy (kJ)
2.4 protein (g)
11.4 carbohydrate (g)
3.3 fat (g)
1.7 saturated fat (g)
1.1 fibre (g)
4.7 sugars (g)

page 80 / makes 16
chewy date bars

139 energy (kcal)
587 energy (kJ)
2.5 protein (g)
26.3 carbohydrate (g)
3.2 fat (g)
1.8 saturated fat (g)
1.8 fibre (g)
14 sugars (g)

page 82 / serves 6
apple strudel tray bake

135 energy (kcal)
578 energy (kJ)
1.4 protein (g)
32.3 carbohydrate (g)
0.8 fat (g)
0.1 saturated fat (g)
2.4 fibre (g)
27.5 sugars (g)

page 84 / serves 12
banana loaf

163 energy (kcal)
684 energy (kJ)
3.5 protein (g)
22.4 carbohydrate (g)
7.2 fat (g)
1.1 saturated fat (g)
1.0 fibre (g)
8.8 sugars (g)

page 86 / serves 12
easy apple tea loaf

184 energy (kcal)
777 energy (kJ)
3.9 protein (g)
28.5 carbohydrate (g)
6.8 fat (g)
1.1 saturated fat (g)
1.1 fibre (g)
14.2 sugars (g)

page 88 / serves 12
malt loaf

129 energy (kcal)
548 energy (kJ)
2.8 protein (g)
30.1 carbohydrate (g)
0.4 fat (g)
0.1 saturated fat (g)
1.6 fibre (g)
11.5 sugars (g)

page 90 / serves 8
pizza tray bake

149/63* energy (kcal)
626/271* energy (kJ)
7.0/4.0* protein (g)
23.9/11.8* carb (g)
3.5/0.3* fat (g)
1.4/0* saturated fat (g)
1.5/3.5* fibre (g)
1.1/11.3* sugars (g)
*tomato pizza topping

page 92 / serves 12
jalapeño cornbread

192 energy (kcal)
802 energy (kJ)
8.2 protein (g)
22.2 carbohydrate (g)
8 fat (g)
1.9 saturated fat (g)
0.9 fibre (g)
3 sugars (g)

page 96 / serves 14
rich chocolate cake

134 energy (kcal)
364 energy (kJ)
3.5 protein (g)
19.3 carbohydrate (g)
5.3 fat (g)
2.7 saturated fat (g)
1.7 fibre (g)
9.3 sugars (g)

page 98 / makes 12
strawberry and cream cupcakes

146 energy (kcal)
617 energy (kJ)
3.0 protein (g)
24.1 carbohydrate (g)
4.8 fat (g)
2.6 saturated fat (g)
1.5 fibre (g)
11.0 sugars (g)

page 100 / serves 12
cheat's red velvet cake

224 energy (kcal)
944 energy (kJ)
10.8 protein (g)
33.4 carbohydrate (g)
6.1 fat (g)
3.2 saturated fat (g)
2.1 fibre (g)
17.2 sugars (g)

page 102 / makes 8
chocolate choux buns

167 energy (kcal)
702 energy (kJ)
4.5 protein (g)
20.5 carbohydrate (g)
8.1 fat (g)
4.4 saturated fat (g)
0.6 fibre (g)
10.3 sugars (g)

page 104 / makes 20
mini celebration cakes

227 energy (kcal)
964 energy (kJ)
3.6 protein (g)
45.3 carbohydrate (g)
4.7 fat (g)
0.7 saturated fat (g)
1.3 fibre (g)
35.2 sugars (g)

page 106 / serves 12
strawberry cream sponge

134 energy (kcal)
562 energy (kJ)
4 protein (g)
18 carbohydrate (g)
5.5 fat (g)
2.7 saturated fat (g)
0.8 fibre (g)
10.7 sugars (g)

page 108 / serves 8
vanilla custard slice

250 energy (kcal)
1053 energy (kJ)
4.3 protein (g)
43.1 carbohydrate (g)
7.6 fat (g)
3.9 saturated fat (g)
0.2 fibre (g)
23.8 sugars (g)

page 110 / makes 12
black bottom cakes

93 energy (kcal)
393 energy (kJ)
3.6 protein (g)
12.2 carbohydrate (g)
3.7 fat (g)
1.9 saturated fat (g)
1.2 fibre (g)
6.5 sugars (g)

page 112 / serves 10
scandi salmon cheesecake

260 energy (kcal)
1086 energy (kJ)
26.7 protein (g)
6.6 carbohydrate (g)
14.2 fat (g)
7.4 saturated fat (g)
0.1 fibre (g)
3.9 sugars (g)

page 116 / serves 6
dutch apple cake

198 energy (kcal)
835 energy (kJ)
6 protein (g)
35.8 carbohydrate (g)
4.4 fat (g)
1.1 saturated fat (g)
1.9 fibre (g)
23.1 sugars (g)

page 118 / serves 6
white chocolate and raspberry cheesecakes

217 energy (kcal)
907 energy (kJ)
8.1 protein (g)
15.4 carbohydrate (g)
14.1 fat (g)
0.4 saturated fat (g)
0.8 fibre (g)
10.6 sugars (g)

page 120 / serves 6
plum and almond cake

166 energy (kcal)
704 energy (kJ)
4.6 protein (g)
30.8 carbohydrate (g)
3.6 fat (g)
0.8 saturated fat (g)
2.2 fibre (g)
21.3 sugars (g)

page 122 / serves 6
berry jelly pots

112 energy (kcal)
478 energy (kJ)
2.4 protein (g)
24 carbohydrate (g)
0.4 fat (g)
0.1 saturated fat (g)
1.2 fibre (g)
3.9 sugars (g)

page 124 / serves 6
jam sponge puddings

133/61* energy (kcal)
503/259* energy (kJ)
4.3/2.5* protein (g)
23.6/10.7* carb (g)
3.0/1.2* fat (g)
0.8/0.8* sat fat (g)
1.5/0* fibre (g)
15.4/6.9* sugars (g)
*low-fat custard

page 126 / serves 12
chocolate amaretti cheesecake

125 energy (kcal)
523 energy (kJ)
2 protein (g)
9.8 carbohydrate (g)
5 fat (g)
2.3 saturated fat (g)
0.3 fibre (g)
5.6 sugars (g)

page 128 / serves 10
lemon and blueberry cheesecake

222 energy (kcal)
927 energy (kJ)
11.2 protein (g)
16.4 carbohydrate (g)
12.6 fat (g)
6.4 saturated fat (g)
0 fibre (g)
13.5 sugars (g)

page 130 / serves 6
fresh fruit flan

144 energy (kcal)
609 energy (kJ)
6.6 protein (g)
23.9 carbohydrate (g)
3.1 fat (g)
0.8 saturated fat (g)
1.6 fibre (g)
15.3 sugars (g)

page 134 / makes 26
crispbread crackers

41 energy (kcal)
174 energy (kJ)
1.1 protein (g)
9 carbohydrate (g)
0.3 fat (g)
0 saturated fat (g)
1.3 fibre (g)
0.1 sugars (g)

page 136 / makes 8
pitta bread

187 energy (kcal)
792 energy (kJ)
5.8 protein (g)
38.2 carbohydrate (g)
2.3 fat (g)
0.3 saturated fat (g)
2.1 fibre (g)
1.2 sugars (g)

page 138 / makes 6
easy home-made pizza

310 energy (kcal)
1310 energy (kJ)
15.5 protein (g)
49 carbohydrate (g)
7 fat (g)
2.8 saturated fat (g)
2.8 fibre (g)
1.6 sugars (g)

page 140 / makes 20
italian crispbread

17 energy (kcal)
73 energy (kJ)
0.5 protein (g)
3.9 carbohydrate (g)
0.1 fat (g)
0 saturated fat (g)
0.2 fibre (g)
0 sugars (g)

page 142 / makes 12
chapattis

72/33* energy (kcal)
307/146* energy (kJ)
2.1/5.2* protein (g)
14.1/3.4* carb(g)
1.2/0* fat (g)
0.2/0* saturated fat (g)
1.5/0.3* fibre (g)
0.3/3.3* sugars (g)
*apple, cucumber and mint dip

page 144 / makes 8
tortilla wraps

114 energy (kcal)
482 energy (kJ)
2.5 protein (g)
20.4 carbohydrate (g)
3.1 fat (g)
0.4 saturated fat (g)
1.1 fibre (g)
0.4 sugars (g)

page 148 / 24 slices
very light white

72 energy (kcal)
306 energy (kJ)
2.4 protein (g)
15.8 carbohydrate (g)
0.4 fat (g)
0 saturated fat (g)
0.9 fibre (g)
0.3 sugars (g)

page 150 / serves 12
foccacia

94 energy (kcal)
400 energy (kJ)
2.8 protein (g)
20 carbohydrate (g)
0.9 fat (g)
0.1 saturated fat (g)
1.1 fibre (g)
0.6 sugars (g)

page 152 / serves 14
soda bread

104 energy (kcal)
441 energy (kJ)
3.8 protein (g)
22.1 carbohydrate (g)
0.6 fat (g)
0.2 saturated fat (g)
1.7 fibre (g)
1.8 sugars (g)

page 154 / serves 10
leek and cheese bread

171 energy (kcal)
726 energy (kJ)
7.2 protein (g)
33.3 carbohydrate (g)
1.9 fat (g)
0.8 saturated fat (g)
2.8 fibre (g)
3.3 sugars (g)

page 156 / makes 10
english muffins

147 energy (kcal)
622 energy (kJ)
5.3 protein (g)
28 carbohydrate (g)
2.3 fat (g)
1 saturated fat (g)
1.4 fibre (g)
2.3 sugars (g)

page 158/ serves 12
no-knead bread

118 energy (kcal)
500 energy (kJ)
3.9 protein (g)
25.7 carbohydrate (g)
0.6 fat (g)
0.1 saturated fat (g)
1.4 fibre (g)
0.5 sugars (g)

page 160 / makes 30
breadsticks

26 energy (kcal)
110 energy (kJ)
1 protein (g)
5.3 carbohydrate (g)
0.2 fat (g)
0.1 saturated fat (g)
0.3 fibre (g)
0.1 sugars (g)

page 164 / makes 12
baked doughnuts

113/119*/132 energy (kcal)**
447/505*/561** energy (kJ)
3.0 protein (g)
19.9/21.6*/25** carb (g)
2.9 fat (g)
1.5 sat fat (g)
0.9 fibre (g)
4.4/6.1*/9.3** sugars (g)
*cinnamon sugar
**iced

page 166 / makes 10
**lightly fruited
teacakes**

214 energy (kcal)
907 energy (kJ)
6.1 protein (g)
38.5 carbohydrate (g)
5.1 fat (g)
2.6 saturated fat (g)
1.8 fibre (g)
10.1 sugars (g)

page 168 / makes 6
orange babas

185 energy (kcal)
770 energy (kJ)
5.2 protein (g)
24.3 carbohydrate (g)
6.6 fat (g)
3.0 saturated fat (g)
0.9 fibre (g)
9.7 sugars (g)

page 170 / serves 8
giant crumpet

100 energy (kcal)
425 energy (kJ)
3.5 protein (g)
20.7 carbohydrate (g)
0.9 fat (g)
0.3 saturated fat (g)
1.0 fibre (g)
1.9 sugars (g)

page 172 / makes 8
**chocolate
breakfast rolls**

147 energy (kcal)
619 energy (kJ)
4.4 protein (g)
29 carbohydrate (g)
2.3 fat (g)
1.1 saturated fat (g)
1.1 fibre (g)
7.7 sugars (g)

page 174 / makes 12
easy iced buns

108/123* energy (kcal)
456/521* energy (kJ)
3.0/3.0* protein (g)
24.3/27.4* carb (g)
0.6/1.0* fat (g)
0.1/0.3* sat fat (g)
0.7/0.7* fibre (g)
9.4/10.7* sugars (g)
*lemon iced buns

index

First published in Great Britain in 2016
by Orion Publishing Group Ltd
Carmelite House
50 Victoria Embankment
London, EC4Y 0DZ
An Hachette UK Company

10 9 8 7 6 5 4 3 2

Text © Justine Pattison 2016
Design and layout © Orion 2016

A CIP catalogue record for this book is available
from the British Library.
ISBN: 978 1 4091 5477 8

Designer: Smith & Gilmour
Photographer: Cristian Barnett
Props stylist: Claire Bignell
Creative director: Justine Pattison
Nutritional analysis calculated by: Lauren Brignell
Recipe assistants: Rebecca Roberts, Jane Remington,
Annie Simpson, Emma Hawkins
Kitchen assistants: Jess Blain, Emily PB
Project editor: Jillian Young
Copy editor: Elise See Tai
Proofreader: Mary-Jane Wilkins
Indexer: Rosemary Dear

Printed and bound in Italy

*Every effort has been made to ensure that the
information in this book is accurate. The information
will be relevant to the majority of people but may not
be applicable in each individual case, so it is advised
that professional medical advice is obtained for
specific health matters. Neither the publisher nor
author accept any legal responsibility for any personal
injury or other damage or loss arising from the use or
misuse of the information in this book. Anyone making
a change in their diet should consult their GP,
especially if pregnant, infirm, elderly or under 16.*

MIX
Paper from
responsible sources
FSC® C015829
FSC
www.fsc.org

www.orionbooks.co.uk

Acknowledgements

Firstly, huge thanks to everyone who enjoys my recipes
and the way I cook. You have given me such fantastic
feedback; I hope you like these dishes just as much.

An enormous thank you to my family; John, Jess and
Emily, for greeting each new recipe enthusiastically,
even when you'd been given nothing more than cakes
for over a month!

I'm truly grateful to the very talented photographer
Cristian Barnett for wonderful photographs that really
make my food come to life. And the brilliant Claire
Bignell for her superb creative skills, selecting the
perfect props and helping make the recipes look
both beautiful and achievable. Massive thanks to
Lauren Brignell for all her invaluable nutritional
support and the hundreds of recipes she has analysed
over the past few months. Also, thanks to Rebecca
Roberts for carefully testing the recipes and assisting
on shoot days. Not forgetting Annabel Wray, Annie
Simpson and Charlotte Page for their hard work in
the test kitchen.

At Orion, I would like to thank Amanda Harris for
believing in this project right from the beginning and
for trusting me to get on and develop the series. Also
thank you to Jillian Young, my fantastic editor, for her
guidance and professionalism and Helen Ewing for
her design support.

A big thank you to everyone at Smith & Gilmour for
making the books look eye-catching, practical and
readable. I'm also grateful to my agent, Zoe King, at
The Blair Partnership, for her constant encouragement
and enthusiasm.

And a final thank you to my family and my friends for
their fantastic support.

Thank you to Kitchen Aid for kindly lending me
their brilliant mixers, blenders and food processors
for recipe testing.